NAPLES, CAPRI
& THE AMALFI COAST
POCKET GUIDE

Walking Eye
mobile app

Discover the world's best destinations with the Insight Guides Walking Eye app, available to download for free in the App Store and Google Play.

The container app provides easy access to fantastic free content on events and activities taking place in your current location or chosen destination, with the possibility of booking, as well as the regularly-updated Insight Guides travel blog: Inspire Me. In addition, you can purchase curated, premium destination guides through the app, which feature local highlights, hotel, bar, restaurant and shopping listings, an A to Z of practical information and more. Or purchase and download Insight Guides eBooks straight to your device.

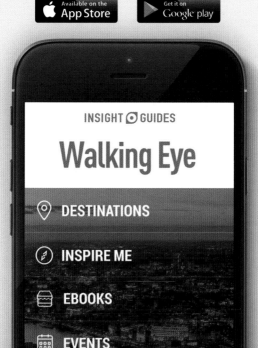

TOP 10 ATTRACTIONS

THE BLUE GROTTO
Capri's most celebrated attraction has been on the tourist itinerary for nearly 200 years. See page 70.

NAPLES' ARCHAEOLOGICAL MUSEUM
An unrivalled collection of ancient sculpture, mosaics and paintings. See page 39.

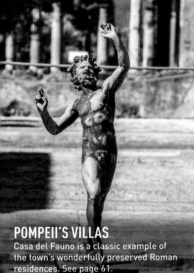

POMPEII'S VILLAS
Casa del Fauno is a classic example of the town's wonderfully preserved Roman residences. See page 61.

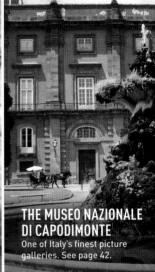

THE MUSEO NAZIONALE DI CAPODIMONTE
One of Italy's finest picture galleries. See page 42.

NAPLES' DUOMO
At the heart of the ancient Centro Storico. See page 35.

POSITANO
One of the most beautiful villages on the Amalfi Coast. See page 83.

VILLA CIMBRONE IN RAVELLO
This clifftop town captivated Wagner, D.H. Lawrence, Greta Garbo and many others. See page 88.

NAPLES, BIRTHPLACE OF THE PIZZA
Still the best place on earth to sample the genuine article. See page 100.

HERCULANEUM
Its ruins have yielded even more treasures than Pompeii. See page 53.

PIAZZA DEL PLEBISCITO
This vast semicircular square is home to the massive church of San Francesco di Paola. See page 25.

A PERFECT DAY

9.00am

Breakfast

Head out for a cappu-
ccino and *cornetto* in
Caffè Scaturchio, on
Piazza San Domenico
Maggiore in the Centro
Storico.

10.00am

Cultural immersion

Take a morning walk
through the Decumani
and Spaccanapoli, visiting
the attractive local
churches, museums,
galleries and shops.

2.00pm

Roman revival

Walk up to the magnificent MANN archaeological
museum, home to the Farnese statue collection
and the treasures of Pompeii, Herculaneum and the
Phlegraean Fields.

12.30pm

Early lunch

Indulge in traditional
wood-fired pizza at
Pizzeria di Matteo (see
page 107), for a taste
that is truly Neapolitan.

4.00pm

Royal ice

Hop on a bus to Piazza
Trieste e Trento,
stopping for cake
or ice cream at the
sybaritic Gran Caffè
Gambrinus (see page
107), before heading
across the square to
see a couple of the
city's most prominent
attractions: the Palazzo
Reale and Castel Nuovo

IN **NAPLES**

8.00pm

Evening at the opera

If it is the opera season and you are extremely lucky, perhaps you will get tickets for the Teatro San Carlo, one of the world's great opera houses. You can also take a guided tour to learn about this spectacular building and its perfect acoustics.

6.30pm

Vomero vista

Walk along Via Chiaia – the city's trendiest shopping street – to the funicular and head up the cliff. Find a neighbourhood bar and settle down with a Campari or martini to watch the sunset across the bay.

8.00pm

Fine dining

Alternatively, enjoy the best of Italian food at one of the city's fabulous restaurants, such as Amici Miei (see page 106), for a lingering dinner.

10.00pm

Jazz club

Finish off your evening in Cammarota Spritz (see page 96) followed by a stroll along the Lungomare, listening to the moonlit waves whispering of Santa Lucia (a song dedicated to this area in Naples).

CONTENTS

INTRODUCTION

Naples is a theatre. Its buildings are arranged on hillsides like box seats encircling a stage. And what a set! Viewed from the heights, a castle seems to plunge like a ship into the waves of a blue sea; there's a sail or two on the water; the coastline curls past the purple cone of Vesuvius towards Sorrento's cape, and Capri floats in a distant haze. Add a little mandolin music and the curtain goes up on Act I. The good news is, the curtain never comes down.

For all its social problems, Naples is a city of incredible beauty and vitality. The noise, chaos and dilapidated areas are impossible to ignore, but for each crumbling tenement block there's a magnificent Baroque church or ancient monument. The food, particularly the pizza, is unforgettable. However, the main draw is the street theatre laid on by the exuberant Neapolitans. Nothing beats just losing yourself in the crowded ancient streets and absorbing all the sights, smells and sounds. And when you've reached sensory overload, you can escape to the nearby islands and coastal resorts.

Divided opinion

Writer Peter Nichols once declared: 'Neapolitans still reproduce what must be the nearest equivalent to life in classical times. Naples is one of the great tests. Some people hate it and some people love it.' He added: 'I think that people who do not like Naples are afraid of something.'

From Naples it is a short ferry ride to Capri, Ischia and the Amalfi Coast. Most holidaymakers hurry straight to the docks and only glimpse Naples in transit to these siren lands, or on a day trip to Pompeii and Vesuvius. They forget that Naples is one of Europe's oldest and greatest cities, the capital of an ancient kingdom and the one-time goal of all would-be sophisticates making the Continental 'Grand Tour'.

The vitality behind the poverty and the beauty amid the squalor have always been part and parcel of the contradictions of Naples. It may come as a surprise to find that its treasures are all still here and that Naples is experiencing renewed popularity among Italians and foreigners alike.

COLOURFUL CAMPANIA

Campania is justly praised for being spectacularly beauti-

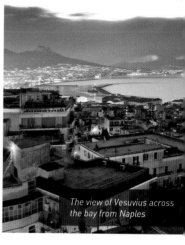

The view of Vesuvius across the bay from Naples

ful. As the region's capital, Naples rules over what was once the Romans' Riviera, a region that remains devoted to the hedonistic pleasures and luxuries once found in Pompeii and Herculaneum. These delights are never more seductive than today in the *dolce far niente* of jet-set 'fishing villages' and café terraces set high above the azure sea. The Ravello that captivated Wagner in the 19th century, wooed Garbo with the same allure in the 20th. The Sorrento that Caruso loved still echoes his serenade. The Positano where Steinbeck found his 'dream place' is every bit as charming today.

Campania is also famous as the birthplace of the pizza; as the unchallenged champion of pasta, with sauces based on plump tomatoes grown in rich volcanic soil; and as the home of irresistible ice creams and pastries. If you overindulge in the wonderful food of the region, a cure is at hand: the fires that smoulder beneath Vesuvius heat the waters and radioactive mud of Campania's spas, renowned for their healing properties for more than 2,000 years.

Much of Campania is volcanic: a dramatic landscape scarred by the escarpments and basins of old craters. It still leaks steam at the seams and is shaken from time to time by tremors. Vesuvius preserved for posterity the cities of Pompeii and Herculaneum by burying them in AD79. It last erupted in 1944, and hasn't finished yet.

FIERY CITIZENS

The people can be volcanic, too. A group on a street corner, whose voices and gestures seem to verge on mayhem, may just be having a friendly chat. Neapolitan hand and body language can communicate hundreds of messages without words. The Neapolitan shrug – meaning anything from 'Who knows?' to 'What do you expect me to do about it?' – is the world's greatest shrug. This is some of the best people-watching in Italy – and that's really saying something.

⊙ NAPLES-SPEAK

The local dialect is more like a language unto itself and can be incomprehensible to Italians from the North – or just about anywhere that is not Naples. The cadence is unique, word endings tend to drop off and diminutives are added to everything. Naples' rich heritage under Spanish and French rule becomes obvious.

Having served (and outwitted) many foreign rulers, the working people of Naples and the surrounding region have evolved a practice of flattery that is totally tongue-in-cheek. Almost any reasonably well-dressed male adult will be called '*dottore*' (ie, a person with a university degree, not a doctor of medicine). A little grey hair will earn the title '*professore*'. Locally, a man of power and/or dignity may be addressed as '*don*', a tradition from the Spanish era. Unfortunately, none of the above can always be taken to imply genuine respect, given the Neapolitan's penchant for a cynical nature.

Negotiating the city is not as fraught with danger as some people, including Neapolitans, would have visitors believe. There are areas that are indeed no-go areas for tourists (the run-down districts of Forcella and Ponticelli, for example), but most of Naples is no more threatening than any other major city.

The southerner's loyalty is to the family. Restaurants are full of three- and four-generation family gath-

The stunning Amalfi Coast

erings. On Sundays young couples with children will be seen carrying neatly packaged pastries and bunches of flowers on their way to visit *la nonna* – Grandma. Graves are regularly tended and decorated with flowers. Many a family is supported by the remittances of a member working in Turin or Brooklyn.

Unemployment in the Mezzogiorno ('Midday'), as the South is known, is almost twice the national average. Naples itself is notorious for poverty, crime, congestion and inefficient services, and when its sons and daughters leave home to find work in the North and abroad, the proud claim *Vide Napoli e poi morí* – 'See Naples and die' – has a sardonic rather than a boastful ring.

But consider, too, the amazing history experienced by this region. Instead of a freeze-frame of a moment in the past, as captured in Pompeii, this is a living, brawling family, proud of its genealogy and its heirlooms, still growing, hospitable, but struggling to make ends meet, in a way that is unique to the Neapolitans.

A BRIEF HISTORY

Naples' history begins in the 8th century BC, when Greek colonists established a settlement on the Pizzofalcone hill and named it after the siren Parthenope. It became an important trading post in the Mediterranean and over the course of a century developed into a model Greek city. The Greeks gradually gained control of the whole region and founded Neapolis nearby. By 400BC the 'new city' had become the thriving commercial and intellectual capital of Campania, the northernmost province of Magna Graecia.

Meanwhile, the Romans were busy expanding their own empire and in 326BC they conquered Naples. Soon almost the entire Italian peninsula was under their control. Impressed by what the Greeks had achieved, the Romans absorbed and adapted Hellenic culture. During the 1st century AD, the bay area became fashionable among wealthy and aristocratic Romans, who built holiday homes and health spas. Emperor Nero had a beachside residence in Baia. Roman poets Ovid, Virgil and Horace were drawn to the south, inspired by its landscapes and the remnants of Greek culture. Pompeii and Herculaneum were two such thriving towns until they were buried by the eruption of Vesuvius in AD79.

Imperial residence

Emperor Tiberius built a huge villa on the isle of Capri, from where (between orgies) he ruled the Roman Empire for 10 years.

Germanic tribes poured into Italy after the Imperial capital was moved from Rome to Byzantium in 330, and the empire divided into east and west. The Goths sacked Rome in 410 and ravaged all Campania.

There was more of the same from the Vandals in 455. Emperor Romulus Augustulus fled to Naples, where he died in 476 leaving no successor. Thus, the Western Roman Empire effectively came to an end in Naples.

In due course, the Eastern Roman Empire of Byzantium allowed Naples to elect its own Dux (duke). The city became rich: churches and houses were built, while art and culture flourished.

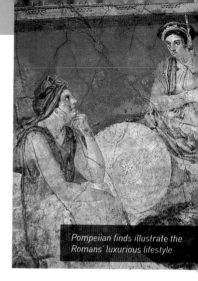

Pompeiian finds illustrate the Romans' luxurious lifestyle

South of Naples, another coastal town was prospering. In the 9th century, Amalfi emerged as an independent merchant republic. While Naples and Amalfi thrived, the rest of the south had been left exhausted and vulnerable – easy prey for the Germanic Lombards who had been busy rampaging across northern Italy. Over the following decades, control of the south was divided between Byzantine rulers and the Lombards.

NORMANS AND GERMANS

In the 11th century, Norman crusaders returning from Palestine started to settle in southern Italy. A century later, Byzantine rule had been eliminated and most of southern Italy was under Norman control. The Norman period of rule was one of relative peace and prosperity. However, the stability of the region was shaken in 1189 by the death of William II, King of Sicily, and the ensuing power struggle between his bastard cousin Tancred and Henry VI of Hohenstaufen.

Henry finally conquered the Sicilian Kingdom and Naples in 1194. The Neapolitan people showed little liking for their new monarch, but their hostility changed to enthusiasm under the rule of his son Frederick II. Born and bred at the crossroads of the Byzantine, Arab and Norman cultures, Frederick was tolerant in his politics. His court in Palermo became a centre for writers, artists and scientists. Frederick also did great things for Naples. He completed the Castel Capuano and Castel dell'Ovo and founded the University of Naples.

After Frederick's death in 1251, Hohenstaufen rule disintegrated. In 1268 Charles of Anjou, brother of the French king Louis IX, took control of the Kingdom of Naples and Sicily and set up his court at Naples. The Angevin kings were keen to re-establish Naples as a cultural capital and during their period of rule a wealth of churches and monuments were built; including the Castel Nuovo, the monastery of San Martino, the cathedral and Santa Chiara church. Robert the Wise, the most powerful of the Angevin rulers, filled his court at Castel Nuovo with theologians, scientists, astrologers, monks and artists – Giotto among them. The Angevins maintained control one way or another until 1435, a period punctuated by Sicilian rebellion and a protracted, desultory war with the Aragons of Spain.

SPANISH VICEROYS

During the late 15th and early 16th centuries the Italian peninsula was in a constant state of turmoil, first through bloody rivalry between France and Spain, and then in the battles to repulse Turkish invasions. Naples was a pawn in these struggles. Spanish rule gained a strong foothold in 1504, when King

The Baroque Palazzo Reale, built under Spanish rule

Ferdinand of Spain (who sponsored Columbus) made his military chief, Gonzalo de Cordoba, 'El Gran Capitan,' viceroy in Naples. There followed a succession of some 60 viceroys until 1734. Pedro de Toledo, viceroy from 1532–53, cleaned up the city, installing sewers, pushing back the walls and carving out the central boulevard that bears his name today.

Perhaps because of Spanish clericalism, the humanising spirit of the Renaissance was slow to arrive in Naples; at the same time, however, the tolerant Neapolitans prevented the Spanish Inquisition from taking hold. Spain's artistic influence can be seen in the Baroque architecture of many of the churches and palaces, including the magnificent Palazzo Reale and a (then) new university that now houses the National Museum.

The viceroys ruled as absolute monarchs and exacted heavy taxes on everything that came and went through the city

Charles III brought to Naples one of Europe's finest collections of art and antiquities, and added further to it by supporting the first excavations of Pompeii and other sites.

gates. In 1647, discontented Neapolitan liberals engineered an uprising, ostensibly led by a fisherman named Tommaso Aniello (known as Masaniello), who proclaimed the Parthenopean Republic, with himself *generalissimo*. This was going too far for his backers. Masaniello was assassinated and the revolt was quashed the following year. Then in 1656 the unhappy city was hit by a plague that killed around 400,000 people in six months.

From 1701–14, all of Europe became embroiled in the War of the Spanish Succession, to decide whether French Bourbon or Austrian Habsburg claimants should take the vacant throne in Spain. Philip V, a Bourbon, was eventually crowned in Madrid, but Naples was passed by treaty to Habsburg Austria. Viceroys appointed by Austria governed the city until 1734, when Philip's son Charles chased them out and entered Naples to wild rejoicing as Charles III. The first of the Bourbon kings of Naples and Sicily, his realm comprised the lower half of the Italian boot, Sicily, Sardinia and the smaller islands. He built splendid palaces at Caserta and Capodimonte, as well as the prestigious San Carlo opera house. His Naples was a brilliant capital, a thriving port, and one of the largest cities of Europe.

REVOLUTION AND UNIFICATION

Charles's successor Ferdinand IV had to flee to Sicily in 1806, when Napoleon sent an army to put his brother Joseph on the throne of Naples. Two years later, Napoleon promoted Joseph to King of Spain and replaced him in Naples with his brother-in-law, Joachim Murat. The English fleet took Capri briefly and bombarded Ischia.

After the fall of Napoleon and Murat, Ferdinand was restored to power, this time as Ferdinand I of the Kingdom of the Two Sicilies. Three more Bourbon kings followed – Francesco I, Ferdinand II, and Francesco II – all noted for their misrule and their complete disregard of the changes sweeping Europe. In 1848 Ferdinand II responded to agitation for more democracy by creating a constitutional parliament and then throwing its leading members in jail. These events prompted Prime Minister Gladstone's famous condemnation of the Bourbon regime as 'the negation of God erected into a system of government'.

When Giuseppe Garibaldi landed in Sicily in May 1860 with his One Thousand (fighters for Italian unification), he had no difficulty in defeating the Bourbon troops, and his own small army grew as it rapidly advanced toward Naples. Francesco II, king for barely a year, fled as the city turned out *en masse* to welcome Garibaldi. A plebiscite overwhelmingly approved the union of Naples and Sicily with the new Kingdom of Italy under King Vittorio Emanuele II of Savoy.

Giuseppe Garibaldi, 'the father of modern Italy'

MODERN TIMES

New Year fireworks display

Under Mussolini southern Italy was a place of exile, something of an Italian Siberia. In 1943, during World War II, Allied armies landed at Salerno. Naples was bombed frequently, and upon departure the retreating German army burned the city's ancient archives. The harbour became an important supply link for the Allied forces – and a bonanza for Neapolitan smugglers and black marketeers. Caserta became the Allied headquarters. While Mussolini and the Germans held Rome and the north of Italy, the south joined the Allies as a 'co-belligerent' under Marshall Badoglio. After the war, traditionally monarchist Naples voted against the creation of the Republic of Italy.

In an effort to alleviate the poverty of the region, the *Cassa per il Mezzogiorno*, the Fund for the South, was created during the 1950s. Factories, steel mills and power plants were built, the *autostrada* network of roads was extended, swampy lands were drained, and agricultural methods were modernised. However, many of the attempts at industrialisation have failed, and the worldwide decline in shipping has reduced the port's commercial importance. Meanwhile, the ancient criminal brotherhood, the Camorra, older than the Mafia, still thrives on racketeering and narcotics. Fighting between rival factions is ongoing.

HISTORICAL LANDMARKS

8th century BC Greeks establish a colony at Parthenope.

474BC Greeks found the new city of Neapolis near Parthenope.

326BC Rome conquers Neapolis.

AD26 Emperor Tiberius rules the Roman Empire from Capri.

AD79 Vesuvius erupts, destroying Pompeii and Herculaneum.

476 Last Roman emperor, Romulus Augustulus, dies in Naples.

763 Naples becomes a duchy.

9th century Amalfi becomes a thriving independent republic.

1139 Naples falls to the Normans.

1194 Henry VI of Germany becomes King of Naples.

1266 Kingdom of Naples given to the French Royal House of Anjou.

1442 Alfonso of Aragon conquers Naples and unites it with Sicily.

1495 Charles VII of France conquers Naples and reigns briefly.

1503 Spain defeats France, rules Naples for two centuries.

1688 Large parts of the city destroyed by an earthquake.

1707 The Austrian Habsburgs gain control of Naples.

1738 Austria loses Naples and Sicily to the Spanish Bourbons.

1806–15 Napoleon briefly controls Naples.

1859–60 Italian War of Liberation, led by Giuseppe Garibaldi. Naples becomes part of unified Kingdom of Italy.

1880–1914 More than 2.5 million Italians emigrate to the Americas.

1943 Naples bombed by Allied forces. After a four-day uprising by the people, the German occupying troops withdraw from the city.

1980 Campania struck by earthquake; 3,000 killed.

2005 Opening of two new art centres, MADRE and PAN, in Naples.

2011 Luigi de Magistris, a former anti-mafia prosecutor, becomes the city's mayor.

2012 Allegations of blackmail, extortion and illicit contract tendering surface in relation to the city's waste management.

2013 Naples hosts the Universal Forum of Cultures.

2016 PM Matteo Renzi loses referendum on constitutional changes and resigns; he is replaced by Paolo Gentiloni. De Magistris is re-elected as mayor.

Spanish Quarter, Naples

WHERE TO GO

One of the great advantages of Campania is the concentration of its attractions: art, history, scenery and leisure are all in close proximity. You don't have to choose between seeing Sorrento or Pompeii, or dining alfresco above Naples' harbour. You can do them all in a single day if you want – although travellers soon find themselves succumbing to a more relaxed southern-Italian approach to sightseeing, particularly in summer, when the heat can be as steamy as the city's trademark volcano. If you want to rush around the sights it is advisable to visit in winter or early spring.

Naples and the Neapolitans make up a fascinating, chaotic urban organism; the city itself is a brilliant living museum. Discovering its treasures is an adventure that leads from the famous bay to the heights, through hectic traffic and narrow byways where noisy family life spills out onto the streets. Even tourists looking forward to relaxing at one of the seaside resorts or islands should not miss the Naples experience.

Come prepared to walk, for whether you are in Old Naples, older Pompeii, or even older Paestum, the best way to engage with this vibrant place and its unique spirit is on foot. The following itineraries are designed to help you discover this spirit for yourself.

NAPLES

A four-lane, one-way boulevard ceaselessly hums with traffic as it skirts an arc of the photogenic seafront from west to east. It runs from the bustling ferry docks of Mergellina to the headland of Pizzofalcone where the Greeks laid the foundations of a new town, Neapolis, nearly 3,000 years ago. At the foot of the hill, just off a little peninsula at the centre of the horseshoe-shaped bay, stands the islet fortress of **Castel dell'Ovo** ❶ (Mon–Sat 9am–7.30pm, winter until 6.30pm, Sun 9am–2pm; free), Naples' oldest castle and a good place to begin exploring.

The Greeks originally used the tiny islet on which the castle now stands as a harbour. Later, the Roman general Lucullus had a villa on Pizzofalcone and built an annexe on the rocks offshore where he stored food and wine for his legendary banquets. In the 5th century a monastery was built here, then in the 12th century the Normans transformed it into a fort. The present structure dates from the early 16th century, following its near destruction by the Spanish. Today, the rooms of the castle are used for functions, cultural events and exhibitions, but you can peer into those not in private use, wander around the battlements and enjoy views across the bay. There is a lift partway to the top.

In the shadow of the castle is a small harbour filled with pleasure craft and little fishing boats. The docks and castle walls are lined with seafood restaurants and cafés. This compact area, known as **Borgo Marinaro**, is the hub of the **Santa Lucia** district. The former fishing community, hailed in the quintessential Neapolitan song, is now an obligatory port of call for the hungry tourist and a good place to sample authentic fish dishes.

Opposite the Castel dell'Ovo, the sea-facing Via Partenope is a row of the city's grandest and most historic hotels – the Vesuvio, Santa Lucia and Eurostars Excelsior all offer splendid

A good egg

Castel dell'Ovo gets its name from the egg *(ovo)* supposedly buried in its foundations. The poet Virgil, who was thought to possess powers of divination, warned that if the egg ever broke catastrophe would befall the city.

Naples' oldest castle, the island fortress Castel dell'Ovo

views of the bay and Vesuvius. From the elegant seafront, walk down Via Santa Lucia, which edges the much scruffier back streets of the working class Palinotto district.

ROYAL NAPLES

At the end of Via Santa Lucia, turn left into Via C Console, which opens out into the **Piazza del Plebiscito**. The vast semi-circular square was used as a car park for decades, but it was cleared of traffic during the 1990s clean-up campaign and is now a popular meeting point – its arcades lined with smart bars and artisan shops. The piazza commemorates the incorporation of the Kingdom of the Two Sicilies into the Italian national state in 1860, an event that deprived Naples of its traditional function as a capital. The square is dominated on one side by the Palazzo Reale (Royal Palace) and on the other by the domed church of San Francesco di Paola.

San Francesco di Paola was modelled on the Pantheon in Rome

The grimly imposing **Palazzo Reale ❷** (www.palazzoreale napoli.it; palace: Thu–Tue 9am–8pm, courtyard: until 7pm in summer, 6pm in winter; charge for palace, courtyard is free, gardens closed for restoration) was first built by Spanish viceroys in the early 17th century. However, the palace takes its character from the sojourn of the Bourbon monarchs and of Joachim Murat, who lived here during his short reign as king of Naples with his wife, Napoleon's sister, Caroline Bonaparte. The Savoy king Umberto I installed the statues on the facade. From left to right, they are the Norman Roger I, Frederick II of Hohenstaufen, Charles I of Anjou, Alfonso I of Aragon, the Habsburg–Spanish emperor Charles V, Charles III of Bourbon, Murat and Vittorio Emanuele II of Savoy.

The palace was badly damaged by Allied bombs in 1943 and by the occupying forces. When the Italian government recovered the building, its royal apartments had to be refurbished. They are now arranged as a museum, with paintings and period furniture from various sources. The palace is also home to two further attractions. The first is the **Biblioteca Nazionale** (www.bnnon line.it; Mon–Fri 8.30am–7pm, Sat 8.30am–1.30pm; free with ID card), the largest public library in southern Italy, holding among other treasures a 1485 copy of Dante's *Divine Comedy*, illustrated with Botticelli engravings. The second is the Memus, an archive of memorabilia from the nearby opera house (http://memus. squarespace.com; Tue and–Thu–Sat 9am–5pm; Sun 9am–2pm).

Opposite the palace, the massive church of **San Francesco di Paola** (www.santuariopaola.it; daily Jul–Aug 6.30am–8pm, Apr–Jun, Sep–Oct until 7pm, Nov–Mar until 6pm; free) was built in 1817 and modelled on the Pantheon in Rome. Outside, are two equestrian statues of Ferdinand IV and his father, Charles III of Bourbon, both by Canova.

Backing onto the Palace on Piazza Trieste e Trento is the **Teatro di San Carlo** ❸ (box office: Via San Carlo, 98/F, tel: 0848 002 008; www.teatrosancarlo.it; tours daily 10.30am–4.30pm; charge; opera season from Nov or Dec–May, but with concerts all year). Italy's most prestigious opera house after La Scala in Milan is also the oldest continuously performing opera house in Europe. It was built for Charles III in 1737 in just eight months and rebuilt after a fire in 1816. Though sombre outside, the rich red-and-gold hall interior is dazzling. Rossini, Donizetti, Bellini and Verdi all composed operas for San Carlo.

Opposite, the cavernous, glass-roofed **Galleria Umberto I** was a showcase when it was completed in 1890. Today it is lined with a number of shops and cafés, but remains strangely empty despite the crowded streets outside.

Diagonally opposite the theatre is the lavish Belle Epoque **Gran Caffè Gambrinus** (http://grancaffegambrinus.com), worth visiting for a coffee and cake or an early evening aperitif. Once the

Castel Nuovo, begun in 1279

haunt of writers and artists, it is a perfect, if noisy spot for people-watching.

PORT AND CASTEL NUOVO

Heading east along Via Vittorio Emanuele, you will come to the second castle in our itinerary, standing guard over Naples' harbour. Giant cruise ships dock at the Stazione Marittima, while smaller ferries and hydrofoils that ply between Sorrento and the islands flow in and out of the adjacent Molo Beverello. The **Castel Nuovo** ❹ (Mon–Sat 9am–7pm; free first Sun of the month) – the 'New' Castle of 1279, as opposed to the old Castel dell'Ovo – is commonly called the Maschio Angioino, the Angevin Fortress, because it was begun by Charles I of Anjou. Sandwiched between two of the five grim, grey towers is the ornate white Triumphal Arch commissioned by Alfonso of Aragon in 1442 to commemorate his defeat of the French and entry into Naples. Across the courtyard, the Palatine chapel is all that remains of the original 13th-century structure. The staircase in the far corner leads to the Hall of the Barons featuring a spectacular rib-vaulted ceiling (now the City Council Chamber).

Spread across three upper floors, the **Museo Civico** displays a collection of silver and bronze artefacts and paintings from the 18th to the 20th centuries. Note also the tablet commemorating the uprising of September 1943, when the Germans were expelled from Naples.

CHIAIA

To the right of Piazza del Plebiscito, behind Caffè Gambrinus, **Via Chiaia** skirts the Pizzofalcone hill. This street, lined with boutiques, leads to the elegant **Piazza dei Martiri** and the wealthy district of Chiaia, home to stylish but pricy shops, art galleries and antiques dealers.

A short walk towards the bay leads to the congested **Piazza Vittoria** (commemorating the defeat of the Turkish fleet at Lepanto in 1571) and the entrance to the 1.5km (1-mile) -long **Villa Comunale**. All of Naples comes to stroll or sit in this leafy seafront park on Sundays and summer evenings. In the park, Europe's oldest **Aquarium** (www.szn.it; closed for restoration until at least 2018) is looking its age: the German naturalist Anton Dohrn founded it in 1872. Inside are 200 species of marine life from the Bay of Naples.

The ocean promenade of the park following the *lungomare* (Via Caracciolo) is one of Italy's most panoramic, if you can ignore the traffic. Parallel to this, on the far side of the park, is the fashionable **Riviera di Chiaia**, once popular with English visitors on the Grand Tour.

Halfway down the broad avenue stands the **Villa Pignatelli** ❺ (www.coopculture.it; Wed–Mon 8.30am–5pm, Tue 9am–2pm; free first Sun of the month). The neoclassical villa was built

The Art of the New

Set in a stunning 17th-century building, the Palazzo delle Arti di Napoli (PAN; Via dei Mille 60; Mon, Wed–Sat 9.30am–7.30pm, Sun 9.30am–2.30pm), just north of Chiaia, is a dazzling art gallery with exhibitions, cultural activities and innovative contemporary art. In the heart of Chaia, the Fondazione Plart (Via Martucci 48; www.fondazioneplart.it; Tue–Fri 9am–1pm, 3–6pm, Sat 10am–1pm; closed Aug) is all about plastics and plastic design.

in 1826 for Ferdinand Acton, son of Ferdinand IV's prime minister, John Acton. Later owned by the Rothschilds, it was donated to the city by Rosina Pignatelli, daughter of the Duke of Amalfi. Officially called the Diego Aragona Pignatelli Cortes Museum, it reflects life in high society around the time of the Unification, with a collection of porcelain and paintings, books and music recordings, and a score of late 19th-century carriages.

Piazza della Repubblica bounds the park's western end and marks the beginning of the Mergellina district. From here, palazzo-lined Viale Gramsci leads to the chaotic Piazza Sannazzaro and the port of **Mergellina**: *aliscafi* (hydrofoils) leave from here for the islands and Sorrento. Just beyond the port is a little park lined with good seafood restaurants, less touristy than those of Santa Lucia. Posillipo's hills come close to the seafront here (see page 46).

CENTRO STORICO

The gateway to Old Naples is the shop-lined **Via Toledo**, laid out by the Spanish Viceroy at the edge of the old city in 1536. The lower end as far as Piazza Carità is pedestrianised. Opposite the Galleria Umberto's western entrance is a station for one of the four funiculars to the hilltop Vomero district (see page 44). Flanking the left-hand side is a labyrinth of tiny streets that make up the **Quartiere Spagnoli**, where soldiers were billeted during the centuries of Spanish rule. Today it is still shaking off its reputation as a den of petty crime. The mere mention of the Spanish Quarter conjures images of Vespa-riding purse-snatchers who disappear into the narrow alleys of this crowded district of tenements. Things have improved recently but tourists should enter with caution and without valuables.

From Via Toledo, turn right down Via Armando Diaz, planted with orange trees. A typical example of the architecture of

Mussolini's fascist era is the Central Post Office in Piazza Matteotti, built in 1925. In contrast, at the head of the Via Monteoliveto around the corner, is the 16th-century Renaissance Florentine facade of **Palazzo Gravina**, now the university's School of Architecture (www.unina.it).

Across the street from the Palazzo Gravina in Piazza Monteoliveto, is the plain, grey **Sant'Anna dei Lombardi**. The Piccolomini Chapel to the left of the entrance holds two fine works by Florentine artist Antonio Rossellino – a 1475 marble nativity with lively angels dancing on the stable roof, and the tomb of Maria d'Aragona, a masterpiece of classic sobriety. In the chapel to the right of the altar is Guido Mazzoni's *Pietà* (1492), a remarkably modelled group of eight life-sized terracotta figures. On the right at the rear of the church, the

Guido Mazzoni's remarkable Pietà in Sant'Anna dei Lombardi

stalls of the old sacristy are beautifully backed with early 16th-century *intarsia* work, designs in inlaid wood.

At the end of Calata Trinità Maggiore, the Jesuit church known as the **Gesù Nuovo** ❻ (www.gesunuovo.it; daily 7am–1pm, 4–7.30pm, guided tour third Sat of the month 3–6pm; free) in the piazza of the same name, is effectively the centre of the old city. The unusual diamond-point facade belonged to a 15th-century princely palace and does not prepare you for the opulent blaze of overblown Baroque gold within. The decorative spire in the piazza is a *guglia*, Naples' characteristically flamboyant answer to the obelisks of Rome.

Spaccanapoli

The **Spaccanapoli** district has been at the heart of Naples since Greek and Roman times. The ancient Greek street that crosses the Piazza del Gesù Nuovo has six names along its arrow-straight 5km (3-mile) east–west course (Via Benedetto Croce and Via San Biagio are the two most prominent) but is best known as Spaccanapoli, literally 'Split-Naples'. A walk along its length, wandering off into side alleys and squares, is the quintessential Neapolitan experience. Half-doors, with the upper part open, reveal the tidy interiors of *bassi*, windowless one- or two-room street-level apartments in the 19th-century buildings, each of which may be home to a large family. Doorways and the street become an extension of the *bassi* where family members sit on chairs peeling vegetables, playing cards and conversing in explosive bursts of dialect.

Baroque refits

Naples has almost 400 churches. Regardless of when they were built, they tend to look alike, since most of them were redecorated in the florid Baroque style.

Tilework at Santa Chiara

Just beyond the Piazza del Gesù Nuovo, to the right, looms **Santa Chiara** ❼ (www.monasterodisantachiara.com; Mon–Sat 7.30am–1pm, 4.30–8pm; museum: Mon–Sat 9.30am–5.30pm, Sun 10am–2pm), named for the patron saint of embroidery, sore eyes and, more recently, TV! Its soaring Provençal Gothic nave is a magnificent relic of Angevin Naples, completed in 1328. It too was covered with Baroque plaster and gilt in the 18th century. After American bombs caused a two-day fire that gutted the church in 1943, the rediscovered underlying Gothic lines were kept in the post-war restoration. Fortunately the bombs spared the glorious 14th-century frescoed cloisters, with 18th-century painted majolica tiles, one of the city's most tranquil and photogenic spots.

Past the ancient statue of the Father of the Nile – one of the city's symbols – is **Piazza San Domenico Maggiore**. Its *guglia* (obelisk) commemorates the plague of 1656, which carried off half the population. In the 13th century St Thomas Aquinas lived and taught in the convent attached to **San Domenico Maggiore** ❽ (daily 10am–7pm; free). Recently refurbished, this is one of the largest churches in Naples, with a supposedly miraculous crucifix. The treasury, built to house the hearts of the Aragonese kings who are buried here, now houses royal religious artefacts. The square has some fabulous restaurants and pastry shops.

Patisserie on Via dei Tribunali

Turn left at the square, past the imposing portal of the Palazzo di Sangro, and right into Via F. de Sanctis to find the **Cappella Sansevero** ❾ (www.museosansevero.it; Mon, Wed–Sun 9.30am–6.30pm), the private chapel and burial place of the noble di Sangro family, the Princes of Sansevero. In the 18th century Prince Raimondo, a soldier and obsessive alchemist, had the 16th-century chapel lavishly redecorated. In the crypt are two skeletons meshed in metal veins. They are thought to be the bodies of servants that the eccentric Raimondo experimented on. However, the reason most people visit the chapel is to see the beautifully carved alabaster figure of the *Veiled Christ* (1753), a masterpiece by Giuseppe Sammartino.

Running parallel to Spaccanapoli is **Via dei Tribunali**, flanked by an ancient arcade. In the morning the street is a bustling market, with housewives delving into buckets of fish and vendors displaying produce in stalls that offer the day's best buys from the rich Campanian fields.

Here you'll find the medieval church of **San Lorenzo Maggiore** ❿ (www.sanlorenzomaggiore.na.it; daily 9.30am–5.30pm) and its 17th-century cloister, set back on a platform on the right, where excavations have uncovered parts of the Roman law courts and, below that, Greek shops and workshops of ancient Neapolis. The church has been restored to the

Gothic of the French architects who built the luminous ribbed apse in the late 1200s. Its showpiece is the 14th-century tomb of Catherine of Austria by Tino di Camaino, one of the first and finest Gothic sculptors in Italy.

Linking Via Dei Tribunali with Spaccanapoli (at Via San Biagio dei Librai) is **Via San Gregorio Armeno**. This little street is crammed with shops selling figurines and knick-knacks for Christmas cribs (*presepi*). You will be amazed by some of the hand-made items with their attention to minute detail. The cloister of the adjoining convent of **San Gregorio Armeno** (daily 9.30am–noon; free), with its fountain and orange trees, offers a place of refuge.

The Duomo

North of Via dei Tribunali, on Via del Duomo, is the cathedral of San Gennaro or **Duomo ⑪** (Mon–Sat 8am–12.30pm, 4.30–7pm, Sun 8am–1.30pm, 5–7.30pm; free). The cathedral is a mixture of styles dating back to pre-Christian times – there are more than 100 Greek and Roman granite columns incorporated in the 16

⊘ UNDERGROUND TOURS

There are several fascinating walking tours of subterranean Naples, which take in a mix of secret tunnels, catacombs, underground aqueducts, air raid shelters, archaeological remnants, the metro, some stations beautifully adorned in art and some showcasing archaeological finds from the tunnels – and of course, plenty of ghosts. There is a completely different world down there, not to be missed. Advance booking is essential. Tours take 90 minutes from Piazza San Gaetano 68, near Sao Paolo Church in the Centro Storico (tel: 081-296 944; www.napolisotterranea.org).

Silver reliquary containing San Gennaro's blood

piers of its nave. The first Angevin king, Charles I, began the cathedral in 1272 on the site of a 5th-century church that in turn had replaced a Roman temple.

The oldest portion is actually another church, Santa Restituta, on a lower level entered from the left aisle (closed for restoration at the time of writing). The church was redesigned a number of times, following the disastrous earthquakes of 1349 and 1456. Its massive 1407 doors were incorporated into the present facade, finished in 1905.

On the right side of the cathedral, the **Cappella di San Gennaro** enshrines the relics of the city's revered patron, San Gennaro. On the first Saturday of May, 19 September, and 16 December, two small phials of his coagulated blood (kept in an elaborate silver reliquary) are said to miraculously liquefy. If the blood does not liquefy, disaster is said to strike. The last time the saint did not cooperate was in 1980 – when Vesuvius erupted. Below the cathedral are layers of ancient Greek and Roman Neapolis. Next door, the Museo del Tesoro di San Gennaro (www.museosangennaro.it; daily 9am–6pm) features paintings, silverware and ex-votos dedicated to the saint.

Just north of the cathedral, in Palazzo Donnaregina on Via Settembrini 79, the fabulous **MADRE** ⓓ (Museo d'Arte Contemporanea Donna Regina; www.madrenapoli.it; Mon,

Wed–Sat 10am–7.30pm, Sun 10am–8pm; free Mon) is a shock after all of the Baroque. Housed within a former convent, this modern art gallery, with works by Rauschenberg, Hirst and Warhol amongst many others, is well worth a visit; not least for the architecture by Alvaro Siza, successfully marrying the historic and the contemporary.

AROUND CORSO UMBERTO I

As Via del Duomo descends toward the harbour, it crosses Corso Umberto I, one of the city's major arteries. If you carry straight on, three blocks past the intersection Via Giubbonari passes under a Gothic clock tower into the **Piazza del Mercato**, home of the church of **Santa Maria del Carmine** (www.santuariocarminemaggiore.it; Mon–Sun 6.30am–12.30pm, 4.30–7.30pm; opening hours can vary).

   The market square is laden with history. An executioner's block for condemned nobles and a gallows for commoners were kept here for centuries. Its principal fame dates back to 1647 when the fisherman Tommaso Aniello, 'Masaniello', began the revolt of the first Parthenopean Republic here. It ended when he was shot nearby. The liberals who proclaimed the abortive second republic in 1799 were executed here, too. Thousands of victims of the 17th-century plague were buried in a common grave under the pavement. The church, already in existence in the 12th century, has a special place in the hearts of Neapolitans. A much-venerated 14th-century image of the dark-haired Madonna, 'la Bruna', is enshrined here. On 15 July, the bell tower erupts in

Black-market goods

Forcella is the Naples 'thieves' market', famous during World War II as the clearing house for loot and contraband lifted from the Allied forces.

a shower of fireworks, to simulate the one-time burning of the narrow campanile.

The most colourful outdoor fish market in Naples sprawls along Via Carmignano, beginning behind the church. It is a vibrant, quintessentially Neapolitan scene. Hoses spray octopi to keep them wriggling, crustaceans of all sizes struggle to escape from their baskets, and the haggling of shoppers competes with the cries of vendors in a street-opera din. The street follows the line of old city walls. Through the arch and across the Rettifilo, street stalls of the Forcella market spill over into the alleys around Via Forcella.

Like Corso Umberto I, **Piazza Garibaldi** is a product of the *sventramento*, the 19th-century 'disembowelling' of Old Naples in the interests of sanitation and urban planning. Nevertheless, the district around the main station has a reputation for hustlers and pickpockets. The **Stazione Centrale** (www.napoli centrale.it) is the main transport hub for all trains in the city, with train services to Rome and beyond, the main bus terminal, a metro stop and the Circumvesuviana line to Vesuvius, Pompeii,

◎ CHIUSO

Chiuso (pronounced 'kyoo-zo') is a word you will learn soon after *grazie* and *per favore*. It means closed. Closed for lunch, closed by a strike, closed 'temporarily' for repairs for many years, closed for whatever reasons and however long. Be prepared every day to find that something you hoped to see is *chiuso*. Numerous rooms in the National Museum have been closed for years; others, and not always the same ones, are closed in the afternoons when the rest of the museum is open. Landmark churches listed on the Naples Tourist Bureau itinerary of artistic monuments are often padlocked, or open only a few hours a day.

Herculaneum and Sorrento virtually next door.

A handsome remnant of the old city walls, the **Porta Capuana** adorns the Piazza Capuana north-west of Piazza Garibaldi. Nearby is the city's oldest castle, **Castel Capuana** (Piazza Enrico De Nicola, Via Vincenzo Muzj, San Lorenzo; Mon–Fri 9am–6.30pm; free), first founded in the 12th century. Buses leave every 20 minutes from Piazza Capuana for the Royal Palace of Caserta, the Versailles of Italy (see page 50).

Treasures from Pompeii in the Archaeological Museum

ARCHAEOLOGICAL MUSEUM

The upper levels of Naples have three important museums, a fort, parks, and private villas with sweeping views of the city and bay. Begin halfway up, at the world-class **Museo Archeologico Nazionale di Napoli** ⑬ (www.museoarcheologiconapoli.it; Wed–Mon 9am–7.30pm) at the northern edge of the Centro Storico, next to Piazza Cavour. The museum's unsurpassed collection of antiquities encompasses the best of the treasures found at the Pompeii, Herculaneum and Phlegraean Fields sites, as well as the legendary Farnese collection of Roman statues that Charles III of Bourbon inherited from his mother, Elisabetta Farnese. So unexcelled were its wonders, it became an obligatory stop on any 18th-century traveller's Grand Tour. There is a huge amount to see, and it isn't made easier by the ongoing restoration programme. Visitors have to contend with the constant rear-rangement of galleries and unexpected room closures.

The ground floor is mostly devoted to Roman copies of the work of the greatest sculptors of ancient Greece. The famous **Tyrannicides**, striding to strike, are in fact copies of a copy made in Athens in 440BC to replace the original, taken by Persians. The undisputed highlights of the Farnese collection are the powerful **Hercules** and the grandiose **Farnese Bull**. The latter, miraculously carved out of a single massive block of marble, depicts the legend of Dirce, tied to a bull by Antiope's sons as punishment for trying to murder their mother. Both monumental statues were found in the 16th-century excavations of the Baths of Caracalla in Rome.

⊙ IL CANTO NAPOLITANO

Nostalgia and melancholy, sunshine and sea, love and betrayal are the hallmarks of songs that are as Neapolitan as pizza. The greatest Neapolitan singer of them all, Enrico Caruso, included *O sole mio!* and *Santa Lucia* in his concerts along with operatic arias, and made them familiar worldwide.

Neapolitan singing has an ancient pedigree. Night ser-enades became such a nuisance to the unromantic trying to sleep that King Frederick II issued a decree in 1221 ban-ning the practice. In the 16th century Neapolitan ditties were popular all over Europe. In the 1700s and 1800s, comic ope-ras flowed from Naples. Then café concerts became the rage. The festival of Santa Maria di Piedigrotta, a popular church in Mergellina, became a contest for new popular songs in 1876. First prize in 1880 went to *Funiculi, Funicula*, celebrating the funicular that had opened on Vesuvius. In 1878 *O sole mio!* won the second prize of 200 lire – even Elvis recorded that one.

The displays on the mezzanine floor are centred on the finest mosaics and paintings from Pompeii. Exceptional is the large **Battle of Issus** from the House of the Dancing Faun. Alexander the Great charges bareheaded from the left as Persian soldiers try to turn the horses of Darius's chariot for flight. The original statue of the faun, after which the house was named, is here too. The

The Farnese Bull

Nile Scenes and detailed mosaics of marine creatures in the adjoining room are from the same house.

This is also the location of the Secret Cabinet or **Gabinetto Segreto**. A manned gate leads to two rooms containing more than 200 frescoes, mosaics and explicit fertility symbols and statues. For decades these were kept hidden because they were deemed too pornographic for public viewing (a 2nd-century AD figure of Pan copulating with a goat could explain why).

Upstairs, to the right, look for the treasures from the Villa of the Papyri in Herculaneum. This mansion and its garden were a veritable art gallery. The seated young Mercury was found there, together with the poised bronze racers and the row of muses that lined the garden pool.

Also on this floor are rooms containing domestic items: lamps, mirrors, combs, theatre tickets, shoes, kitchenware, charred food, the instruments from Pompeii's House of the Surgeon, and the beautiful 115-piece silver service from the House of Menander. The top floor is given over to a hoard of Greek and Etruscan pottery, as well as the museum's collection of coins.

Just south of the museum is the finely restored **Galleria Principe di Napoli**, an architect's hymn of praise to shopping. Also nearby, the **Accademia di Belle Arti** (Via Santa Maria di Costantinopoli; www.abana.it/it/patrimonio/galleria; Tue–Sat 10am–2pm; free) has a fine collection of 17th–20th century art. South of this on Via Santa Maria di Costantinopoli is the pretty Piazza Bellini, with its literary cafés and statue of the great composer. Beyond this, head through the covered Porta d'Alba with its bookshops to **Piazza Dante**, an elegant but busy piazza at the end of Via Toledo, home to fast food, metro and bus termini.

THE CATACOMBS AND CAPODIMONTE

Catch a bus uphill from the Museum or Piazza Dante to the **Catacombe di San Gennaro** (www.catacombedinapoli.it; Mon–Sat 10am–5pm, Sun 10am–2pm, hourly guided visits only). Get off at the domed Madre del Buon Consiglio church where the road doubles back sharply just below Capodimonte. The ticket booth for the catacombs is to the left of the church. The first tombs cut into the rock here were for pagan, 2nd-century Roman families of nobility. Christians probably began using them a century or so later. The arched halls and rooms on two levels are decorated with mosaics and frescoes that date back to the 6th century.

Crowning the hill at the end of Via Capodimonte, in a vast park that once served as a royal hunting ground, is the **Museo Nazionale di Capodimonte** ⓮ (www.museocapodimonte.beniculturali.it; Thu–Tue 8.30am–7.30pm), an oasis of calm and fresh air. Charles III built the palace in 1738 to house his picture collection. He also built the Capodimonte porcelain works in the grounds, its extravagantly ornate and delicate output becoming famous throughout Europe. There is plenty of porcelain still in the palace, whose sprawling chambers also house one of the finest picture galleries in southern Italy. On the first floor, the Farnese collection includes such masterpieces as Masaccio's *Crucifixion*, Botticelli's *Madonna and Child with Angels*, an early Renaissance treasure, *Antea* by Parmigianino, the portrait of a young woman thought to be the artist's lover, and the monumental

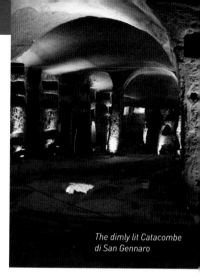

The dimly lit Catacombe di San Gennaro

canvases by the Carraccis. Raphael is represented by his portraits of *Leo X* and *Two Cardinals and Cardinal Alessandro Farnese*. Pride of place is given to Titian's *Danaë* (1545).

The **Galleria delle Cose Rare** contains a sparkling display of precious objects that once graced the Farnese palaces. The rooms beyond contain **Flemish paintings**, most of which were acquired by the Bourbons at the beginning of the 17th century when the Netherlands was enjoying an artistic golden age. Wander through the ornate **Royal Apartments**, and marvel at the magnificent ballroom with its giant chandelier, and the Porcelain Parlour of Queen Maria Amalia, lined with over 3,000 tiles made in King Charles's porcelain factory.

The second floor is given over to Neapolitan art from the 13th to the 18th centuries. Among the early works is Simone Martini's *San Ludovico di Tolosa* (1317), a masterpiece of Italian Gothic art from San Lorenzo Maggiore. Central to the

17th-century works in the collection are the Caravaggio canvases, in particular the *Flagellation of Christ* (1607–10). The third floor is dedicated to modern and contemporary art. The star exhibit here is Andy Warhol's *Vesuvius*.

VOMERO

The Vomero district is on another hill, reached from the seafront and centre of Naples by funicular. The three stations are at the foot of Via Toledo on the tiny Piazza Duca d'Aosta; on Piazza Montesanto across Via Toledo from the Piazza Dante; and in the Chiaia district at Piazza Amedeo. The Montesanto funicular comes closest to the Castel Sant'Elmo, but they all arrive within close walking distance of each other.

The hilltop citadel of Naples, the imposing **Castel Sant'Elmo ⑮** (www.coopculture.it; Wed–Mon 8.30am–7.30pm; free first Sun of the month) is a sombre and brooding presence when seen from below, but a breeze-swept platform for admiring the 360-degree view from its ramparts. Originally built in 1275, King Robert of Anjou enlarged the castle on this strategic spot in 1349, but its current form dates from the 16th century. It is also now home to the **Museo del Novecento**, focusing on Neapolitan artists of the 20th century.

Below the castle is the **Certosa e Museo di San Martino** (www.coopculture.it; Thu–Tue 8.30am–7.30pm; free first Sun of the month), a former Carthusian monastery and now museum of Neapolitan history and culture. The monastery was founded in 1325 by Charles d'Anjou, but it was given a Baroque makeover in the 16th and 17th centuries, when dozens of Neapolitan-school painters worked on its walls.

From the cloistered entry, proceed past the gold coach to the terraced gardens of vines, pines and paths. From this unique balcony belvedere you will be able to identify the main landmarks of

the city, spread out like a map below. To the right of the little cloister, the Maritime Section exhibits ship models. On the left, steps
descend to the Presepe Cuciniello, the champion of all Neapolitan
cribs. Each of the 177 painted terracotta figures is an exquisite
work of art carved by the popular sculptor Giuseppe Sammartino,
and clothed in hand-sewn period costumes.

Rooms around the main cloister are devoted to the paintings of
Neapolitan artists, costumes, glassware and historical exhibits.
The cloister itself is a restrained, rather Florentine construction,
with a small monk's cemetery, guarded by skulls, in one corner.
Continue through the chapter room of the monastery's church to
see the fine *intarsia* (inlay) work on stalls and cabinets in the sacristy and, in the Treasury Chapel, *Descent from the Cross*, one of
the great masterpieces by José Ribera.

The centre of the Vomero
district is Piazza Vanvitelli,
cut through from east to
west by the shopping street
of Via Scarlatti. The parallel street to the south is Via
Cimarosa, where you will
find the **Villa Floridiana** 🔟
(8.30am–1hr before sunset),
formerly the grounds of the
19th-century Villa Flori-
diana, now a public park.
The royal summer palace
now houses the **Museo
Nazionale di Ceramica
Duca di Martina** (www.
coopculture.it; Wed–Mon
8.30am–2pm). In addition

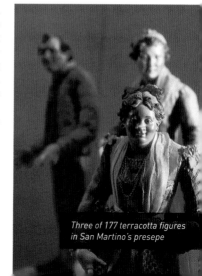

*Three of 177 terracotta figures
in San Martino's presepe*

to the porcelain from the royal Capodimonte factory, this fine collection also has a valuable selection of Meissen, Sèvres, Nymphenburg, Wedgwood and Oriental ceramics and majolica.

POSILLIPO

Long before the Vomero district became fashionable, the seaside suburb of **Posillipo** ⑰, on the northern arm of the bay, was the retreat of the city's rich. Monte Posillipo, rimmed with apartments and villas, slopes gently to the sea, closing the western end of the inner bay. Murat began the Via di Posillipo around this cape in 1812 as a more direct route to Pozzuoli. This panoramic road follows the shore from Mergellina and climbs past parks and faded princely estates, such as the 17th-century **Palazzo Donn'Anna** (open for special events only; www.fondazionedefelice.it). Passing a park with a World War I memorial, the road reaches a crest at the Quadrivio del Capo crossroads. Take the left road down about a kilometer (0.6 mile) to **Marechiaro**. Popular seafood and pizza restaurants ring the tiny harbourside piazza of this former fishing village. Just beyond the Quadrivio, the **Parco Virgiliano**'s belvedere offers splendid views over the bay out to Capri. Directly ahead, attached to the peninsula by a small strip of land, is the island of **Nisida**. Legend has it that Brutus and Cassius hatched their plot to kill Caesar here.

Pursuing pleasure

The Posillipo peninsula was once such an idyllic rural landscape that the Greeks named it *Pausilypon* – 'the soothing of pain'. It is possible that Epicureanism, the philosophy based on the pursuit of pleasure, originated here.

CAMPI FLEGREI

In the days of Imperial Rome the fashionable place to have a holiday villa was along the

Pozzuoli streetlife

northern curve of the Bay of Naples, called the Phlegraean Fields (Campi Flegrei), from the Greek for 'burning fields.' The whole district overlies volcanic fire, dotted with hot springs and 13 small craters, one of which still shoots up clouds of sulphurous steam. Although stripped over the centuries and half-buried by neglect and modern development, through the scattered remains you can still recreate the image of this ancient Roman playground in your mind's eye.

POZZUOLI

The busy town of **Pozzuoli** ⑱ (pop. 82,000), 8km (5 miles) west of Naples, is the starting point for visiting the Phlegraean Fields sites. On a slope behind the harbour, the **Duomo**, the Cattedrale di San Procolo, was just another 17th-century church until a fire in 1964 uncovered the marble walls and cornices of a temple to Augustus, the first emperor to be deified. San Gennaro, Naples' patron saint, found early martyrdom here in AD305. These days, the town's most famous native is Sophia Loren, but it is also well known for its gastronomy.

Set back from the port area are the ruins of a 2nd-century BC *macellum* (market). These splendid ruins were submerged in water until the mid-1980s when the rising of land levels caused by volcanic activity left them uncovered.

The **Anfiteatro Flavio** (www.coopculture.it; Wed–Mon 9am–1hr before sunset) lies beyond the railway station opposite the harbour. It was covered by volcanic material until the 19th century and, as a result, is incredibly well preserved. Built in the 1st century AD, the amphitheatre held 40,000 spectators, and could be flooded for mock naval battles. About half an hour's walk uphill or a short bus ride is the **Solfatara** (www.solfatara.it; daily Apr–Oct 8.30am–7pm, Nov–Mar until 4.30pm), a shallow moonscape crater filled with glaring white ash. You are walking on top of a snoozing volcano, with the stink of sulphur from steaming fumaroles and bubbling mud pits. At the Boca Grande fumarole, steam temperatures are over 160ºC (320ºF). This is where guides light a match at a vent, causing clouds of white ionised vapour to puff from cracks.

One of the more cutting-edge museums in the bay area, the **Città della Scienza**

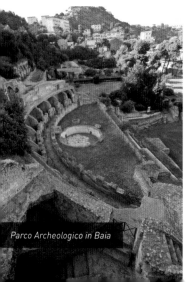

Parco Archeologico in Baia

in Bagnoli (Tue–Sat 9am–3pm, Sun 10am–5pm; www.cittadella scienza.it) hosts a programme of science exhibitions and now houses the new CORPOREA, the first museum in Europe dedicated to the human body as well as a 3D planetarium.

All along the Gulf of Pozzuoli out to its tip at Capo Miseno, Roman buildings that once stood on the shore are submerged, providing great treasure-hunting opportunities for divers.

BAIA

The seaside village of **Baia** ⑲ was once a luxurious holiday resort for wealthy Romans. The **Parco Archeologico** (www.parcoarch eologicosommersodibaia.it; Tue–Sun 9am–1hr before sunset) encloses the ruins of the Imperial Palace and baths, built and added to by the Caesars over 400 years from the 1st century AD. Signage is confusing and the entrance is virtually concealed; the easiest way is a footbridge over the tracks at the railway station. The site, on a cliff with three terrace levels, commands a view over the sea from Capo Miseno on the right, to Pozzuoli, Posillipo, Vesuvius and the Sorrento peninsula to the left. On the coast stood the villas of such illustrious Roman figures as Julius Caesar, Lucullus, Pompey, Cicero, Sulla – a veritable enclave of the rich and famous. Many of these villas are now underwater (tours in glass-bottomed boats are available in summer); others provide walls for houses on the main street between the cliff and the bay. The whole complex was raided by Saracens in the 9th century.

After Baia the road climbs to the **Castello di Baia** (Tue–Sun 9am–2.30pm; free Tue–Fri), a fortress overlooking the Gulf of Pozzuoli, built by the Spanish to defend against the Saracens in the 16th century. The impressive archaeological museum has finds from the Shrine of the Augustali at Miseno (see page 39) and a reconstruction of the submerged nymphaeum found at Epitaffio point, north of Baia port.

Descending to Bacoli, look for signs to the Piscina Mirabilis. This vast covered reservoir carved out of the rock, the largest of its kind, was the terminus of an aqueduct designed to provide water for the Roman fleet at Miseno.

The sheltered harbour at **Capo Miseno** was used as a naval base first by the Greeks then by the Romans. Pliny the Elder

⊙ THE ROYAL PALACE AT CASERTA

Perhaps the most grandiose palace in all Italy lies 28km (18 miles) northeast of Naples. Charles III almost certainly had Versailles in mind when he set out to create the Royal Palace of the Bourbons at Caserta in 1751. It was completed in 1774 by his son, Ferdinand I.

The palace (www.reggiadicaserta.beniculturali.it; Wed–Mon 8.30am–7.30pm) has 1,200 rooms, 1,790 windows and 34 staircases. The architect Vanvitelli's masterpiece is the grand staircase of marble and inlaid coloured stone surmounted by a double elliptical vault. Hidden behind the rim of the lower vault, musicians played to greet the king and his guests. At the top of the stairs Vanvitelli created a theatrical octagonal vestibule of columns, cupolas and arches. To one side, the gorgeous Palatine Chapel gleams in gold, green and white. Scarred antique columns along the sides are from the Serapeum of Pozzuoli. To the rear of the second courtyard is another Vanvitelli gem, the Court Theatre.

The magnificent park (8.30am–1hr before sunset) is worth visiting to see the Cascata Grande, an immense waterfall tumbling down a wooded hill. Shuttle buses run regularly between the palace and the Fountain of Diana at the foot of the 76m (249ft) cascade.

was in command of the fleet here when Vesuvius erupted in AD79, and met his death trying to save fugitives from Pompeii. The famous description of the event by his nephew Pliny the Younger was made from this vantage point. Drive up to the Capo Miseno lighthouse at the top of the headland for one of the best views around.

The tunnel leading to the Sybil's Cave at Cuma

CUMA

The holy of holies of the Phlegraean Fields was at **Cuma ⑳**, about 9km (5.5 miles) from Bacoli, past a sandy bathing beach, the **Marina di Fusaro**. Founded by Greek colonists in the 8th century BC, Cuma became an important city that controlled the Phlegraean Fields region for nearly 500 years, until its decline under the Romans. The **Acropoli di Cuma** (www.coopculture.it; daily 9am–1hr before sunset) is surrounded by farmland studded with ruins, including an amphitheatre.

One of antiquity's most venerated sites is the famous **Cave of the Cumaean Sybil** (Antro della Sibilla), where the prophetess answered questions about life and death and foretold the future. Although it never had the status of Delphi, people came from distant lands to consult the Sybil. The cave is approached through a long keyhole-shaped tunnel lit by windows cut into the hillside.

From the Sybil's cave a Via Sacra paved by the Romans climbs to the ruins of a temple to Apollo. The path extends to the site of a temple to Jupiter, later converted to a Christian church. The old Via Domiziana, which runs back towards Pozzuoli passes under the **Arco Felice**, an arched defile 20m (65ft) high, cut into the rock by the Romans in the 1st century AD.

VESUVIUS

Seen from Naples, it becomes clear that the perfect cone of **Vesuvius** ㉑ is actually a volcano within another, much larger volcano. The crater of the mother mountain, Monte Somma, rings Vesuvius to the left, its slope broken off in an eruption 17,000 years ago. The present 1,276m (4,173ft) cone has grown and changed shape through many eruptions, the most recent in the 1940s.

Earthquakes preceded the 1944 explosion; then a stream of superheated lava roared down the Atrio del Cavallo, the valley between Vesuvius and Somma, travelling at 160kmh (100mph). The road from Torre del Greco skirts this lava flow. It is surprising how quickly vegetation has covered the desolation – in spring the lower slopes are covered with golden broom. In winter the cone often gets a dusting of snow.

The road ends some 275m (900ft) below the volcano's rim. A half-hour walk up a steep path in the loose reddish cinders brings you to the top (ticket booth open 9am–2hrs before sunset; closed in bad weather). Good walking shoes are essential for this hike. Around the

> ## The Golden Mile
>
> Between Herculaneum and Pompeii the Miglio d'Oro (Golden Mile) includes a stretch of fabulous 18th-century villas built around the Reggia, the palace built by King Charles. Several can be visited on a walking tour. Start at Villa Campolieto (Corso Resina 283, Ercolano), where you can pick up a map and audio guide.

crater's edge, where wisps of steam drift from fumaroles, intrepid tourists pose for photos. Landslides have partially filled the inner cavity. The crater is 200m (654ft) deep and 600m (1,962ft) across. Views from up here across the bay are spectacular.

It is certain that Vesuvius will blow its top again one of these days, but it appears now to have entered a dormant cycle after erupting every few years since 1858.

Vesuvius is actually a volcano within another volcano

A 130-year period of inactivity preceded the calamitous eruption of 1631, when 3,000 people were killed, the mountain lost its top, and ashes fell as far away as Istanbul. There were also spectacular eruptions in 1872, 1906, 1929, 1933 and 1944.

HERCULANEUM

Just 12km (8 miles) southeast of the centre of Naples (Ercolano station on the Circumvesuviana line), at the foot of Vesuvius, **Herculaneum** ㉒ (named after its legendary founder Hercules) is delightfully empty of the crowds that inundate Pompeii. With just 5,000 inhabitants, the ancient town of Herculaneum was a smaller, more refined place than its bigger, brasher neighbour. While Pompeii was crushed under falling volcanic debris and red-hot cinders, Herculaneum was filled from the bottom up by ash and pumice carried on a torrent of ground-hugging superheated gas. Roofs did not cave in. The city was simply inundated by a flood that covered it to an average depth of 20m (65ft). This semi-liquid muck cooled and hardened to encase and protect balconies, furniture, food on the tables, and even glass window panes and wax writing tablets. Once discovered, the soft tufa sandstone was relatively easy to carve out. However, modern Ercolano sits directly on top of the site and half of the ancient town remains unexcavated.

EXPLORING HERCULANEUM

It is a 10-minute walk downhill, through the soulless modern town to the excavation site of **Herculaneum** (www.pompeiisites.org or www.coopculture.it; Apr–Oct 8.30am–7.30pm; Nov–Mar 8.30am–5pm; last admission 90 min before closing; free first Sun of the month). The city is laid out in the typical Roman grid pattern, with intersecting streets known as Decumani and Cardi. Beginning at Cardo III, on the left is the large **Casa d'Argo** (House of Argus), with Egyptian-looking columns. On past the intersection of the Decumanus Inferior are the **Terme del Foro** (Forum Baths), with women's and men's sections built around an exercise court. A Neptune whose legs turn into sea serpents decorates the mosaic floor of the tepidarium. Sea creatures painted on the ceiling over the cold plunge were reflected in its water.

East on the decumanus at the corner of Cardo IV is the much-photographed **Casa Sannitica** (Samnite House). The Samnites preceded the Romans here, as in Pompeii, and the house is a dignified structure of the 2nd century BC, one of the oldest in Herculaneum. Across the intersection, the overhanging roof, beams and door-frame of the **Casa del Tramezzo del Legno** (House of the Wooden Partition) are original. Inside, note the cleverly hinged doors that slide on bronze grooves to close off the atrium. A perfectly preserved wooden bed stands in the corner of an adjoining bedroom. A loaf of bread with a bite taken out of it was found in the dining room off the garden where lunch was being served as the disaster struck.

On the east side of Cardo IV above the Samnite House are the Weaver's House, the House of the Charred Furniture, the House of the Neptune Mosaic and the House of the Beautiful Courtyard, all remarkably preserved, with homely bits of everyday belongings, finely fashioned furniture, mosaics and frescoes. This road ends at a broad pedestrian street called the Decumanus Maximus and the edge of the still unexcavated Forum under the modern town. The **Palaestra of Herculaneum**, which extends under the path from the ticket booth, is only partly uncovered. In the centre a cross-shaped pool was fed by water from a bronze serpent coiled around a tree. Apparently games were in progress on the day of the eruption; stone 'shot-put' balls were found in the Palaestra.

The bronze serpent, Palaestra of Herculaneum

The finest houses, at the end of Cardo V, had a view over the sea towards Capri from the embankment overlooking Herculaneum's marina. The grandest is the **Casa dei Cervi** (House of the Deer), where a pair of delicate sculptures of stags attacked by dogs was found. Neighbours to the left occupied the **Casa dell'Atrio a Mosaico** (House of the Mosaic Atrium), with its black-and-white checkerboard pavement that rippled under the shock of the eruption. This house had glassed-in porticos and a solarium looking out to sea.

Steps at the end of Cardo V descend to the small **Terme Suburbane** (Suburban Baths). Light filters into rooms through windows that once were glassed. The tubs, tanks, boilers, and even firewood for furnaces have been left as they were found. A frieze of warriors modelled in stucco decorates the dressing room above marble benches. Panelled wooden doors hang on their original hinges. A heavy marble basin lies on its side where it was tossed by the heaving earth. At the end of a corridor, graffiti in a room for private parties total up the bill for an order of cakes and record the pleasures of a homosexual encounter.

As you climb the steps to leave this small, elegant city, look behind you. The cone of brooding Vesuvius rises over the

⊘ ROMAN REMAINS

Until 1980 only a few bodies had been found in the ruins of Herculaneum, and it was believed that the estimated 5,000 inhabitants had managed to flee to safety. In 1980 came the discovery of hundreds of skeletons of men, women and children who had taken shelter in vaults at the marina. These skeletons provided a rare opportunity to study the size and health of typical individuals, for Romans cremated their dead and cemeteries contain only urns with ashes. Men were on average 1.65m (5ft 7 ins) tall, while women were considerably shorter. Teeth cavities were uncommon, perhaps because Romans did not have refined sugar in their diets.

Romans enjoyed a level of health care not available again until relatively modern times. A kit of instruments found in the House of the Surgeon in Pompeii included scalpels, forceps, catheters, implements for brain and eye surgery, suction cups, scissors, pincers and clamps.

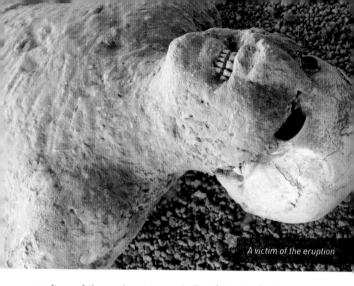

A victim of the eruption

rooftops of the modern town, only 7km (4.3 miles) above you. Beyond Herculaneum the road stretches around the bay to Torre Annunziata, where the glorious **Villa Poppaea** (same opening times as Herculaneum), built by the second wife of Emperor Nero, has some of the finest frescoes yet uncovered. It is a Unesco World Heritage site.

POMPEII

In the 1st century AD, **Pompeii** ㉓ was a prosperous commercial seaport at the mouth of the Sarno River. What happened to the 20,000 citizens in August AD79, was not as sudden as a bomb blast, but just as devastating. There had been warnings, and a bad earthquake 17 years earlier, although Vesuvius was green to its crest with vineyards and had never been considered threatening. Tremors shook the earth for several days in late August. Then

Ruins of the Temple of Venus

around noon on 24 August a mushroom cloud shot up from the mountain and soon obscured the sun. Out of the darkness and growing stench of gas, a torrent of ashes, cinders and pumice pebbles fell on to the surrounding towns and settlements. The earth shuddered repeatedly and tidal waves rolled in from the sea. Worse was to follow as the mushroom cloud collapsed, raining a super-heated pyroclastic flow of rock, ash and dust down on the town, burning and suffocating the terrified citizens. When the sky cleared on 27 August Pompeii was buried under 7m (23ft) of ash. This light material solidified with rain and time, preserving everything it encased in a time capsule.

Pompeii remained hidden until 1594, when workmen tunnelling for an aqueduct unearthed some walls and tablets. Serious excavations were begun in 1748, and most of the statues and valuables were removed in the next 150 years. Much of the treasure is in the Museo Archeologico Nazionale in Naples (see page 39).

Once you have left Naples, you can reach Pompeii in 20 minutes by the *autostrada*. There are frequent trains to the ruins from the Central Station at Piazza Garibaldi (on the Circumvesuviana line). Your hotel or the tourist information office can advise you on where to sign up for a guided tour.

Pompeii's coachloads of visitors and the erosive effects of the elements have led to a series of collapses in recent years; the Italian government put into place a €150 million makeover in 2013 in an attempt to preserve the site's priceless relics. But the real turnaround came when the Great Pompeii Project was put in charge of the renovations. Since then, some parts of the sites have been successfully restored and have reopened to the public.

AROUND THE FORUM

Visits to the **Scavi di Pompeii** (www.pompeiisites.org or www.coopculture.it; excavations daily Apr–Oct 9am–7.30pm, Nov–Mar 9am–5pm; last admission 90mins before closing; free first Sun of the month; ID is required to hire the excellent audio headsets) begin at the Porta Marina, the sea gate, one of eight in the city walls. As with many of Pompeii's main thoroughfares, the Via Marina's lava paving stones are rutted by the passage of cart and chariot wheels.

The road leads past the Tempio di Venere (Temple of Venus) to the **Tempio di Apollo** (Temple of Apollo). The sundial on the pillar to the left of the raised temple is a reference to Apollo's role as god of the sun. A few steps more and you are in the **Foro** (Forum) **A**, Pompeii's commercial and religious centre. At the head of the Forum stands the raised **Tempio di Giove** (Temple of Jupiter). To its right is the central market, the **Macellum**; originally domed, it is divided into stalls for produce vendors and *argentari*, moneychangers. Looming over all, straight ahead is Vesuvius, far from dead and suddenly looking ominous.

Pompeii's populace

The most prominent citizens of Pompeii were newly rich merchants who built showy houses (the Imperial court and Roman aristocrats had their holiday villas at fashionable Stabia, Herculaneum, Neapolis or near Baiae, across the bay). Most of Pompeii's population consisted of working people, artisans, shopkeepers and slaves.

When the disaster struck, many Pompeiians were overcome by poisonous fumes, their lives interrupted by the forces of nature. The wet ash solidified around their bodies like a mould that emptied in time as the flesh decomposed. By filling these 'moulds' with plaster, archaeologists have created lifelike casts of the victims. Several of these are to be seen in the **Horreum**, a sort of shed originally for storing and weighing grain stocked with wine jars and crockery, to the left of the Tempio di Giove. A man crouches, covering his face with his hands; a pregnant woman lies face down.

Across the Forum are several small temples, including one to Vespasian, the emperor who introduced public toilets (there is one at No. 28 on the west side). The buildings on the south end of the Forum served as the 'City Hall,' offices of the municipal council and other dignitaries.

After you see the Forum, there is no obvious itinerary to follow in Pompeii. The orderly Roman rectilinear layout of blocks and streets has been divided by archaeologists into numbered Regions, Insulae (blocks) and houses, but the system is incomplete, changing, and can be confusing to the uninitiated. Start with the **Terme del Foro** ⓑ, a small Roman bath just beyond the cafeteria and left on Via delle Terme. Note the delicate stuccowork on the ceilings.

Passing through the Porta di Ercolano in the northwestern corner, the road descends along the romantic, tree-lined Via dei Sepolcri, flanked by ancient funerary monuments. At the lane's end, to the left, is the **Villa di Diomede** **C** (Villa of Diomedes). The unusually big windows must have made this a sunny house, with pleasant views of the large garden. The body of the owner was found with the garden gate key in his hand and, beside him, a slave carrying a bag of valuables.

REVEALING VILLAS

At this point you can leave the ruins proper, and follow signs to the **Villa dei Misteri** **D** (Villa of the Mysteries). This elegant residence is decorated with the largest and most remarkable wall paintings surviving from Roman times. A sequence of scenes on a glowing red background follows the initiation of a newly married woman into the Dionysian mysteries, an orgiastic rite of Greek origin.

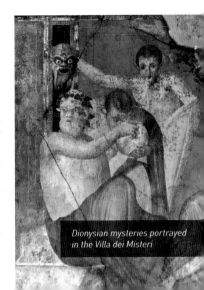

Dionysian mysteries portrayed in the Villa dei Misteri

The most interesting houses are in the area northeast of the Forum. Return to the crossroads above the Temple of Jupiter and follow Via della Fortuna. The second block on the left is entirely taken up by the **Casa del Fauno** **E** (House of the Faun), a luxury villa with four dining rooms, one for each season, two peristyles and a small bath which made clever use of the heat produced by the oven in the adjacent kitchen. Most of the house's treasures, including the mosaic of Alexander and the original dancing faun found in one of the two inner courtyards, are in the Archaeological Museum.

Another block along, in the Vicolo dei Vettii, is Pompeii's most famous house, the **Casa dei Vettii** ❻ (House of the Vettii). Carefully restored, it gives a good idea of how wealthy merchants lived. Paintings in the dining rooms and bedrooms show cupids engaged in typical activities of the town. Just inside the entrance is a fresco of Priapus, god of fertility, weighing his huge penis on a scale against a bag of gold. It used to be covered by a locked panel, and guards made a good income by giving visitors a peek. Now it's out in the open for all to see and giggle at. All over Pompeii you will see phallic symbols on houses. These were to ward off the evil eye, similar to the red coral or plastic amulets worn today in southern Italy.

Bathtime

Visiting the baths was an important part of the Roman daily routine. First comes the vaulted changing room, lined with seats and niches for clothes. Off this are the *frigidarium*, for cooling off after the *tepidarium*, where a brazier heated the air, and the *caldarium*, with a pool and steam from an external boiler. Exercising was done in the adjoining gym, or *palaestra*, and there were separate facilities for women.

BROTHELS AND BATHS

Follow the Vicolo dei Vettii back to the Via della Fortuna and cross to descend the Vico Storto. Note the large bakery with mills on the left. Grain was poured in the top cylinder and the millstone turned by donkeys or slaves. Wind around to the left on Via degli Augustali to the Vicolo del Lupanare. Here, a series of small paintings illustrate the services offered in this rather cramped two-storey brothel, the **Lupanar Africani et Victoris**. Across the street, the doorway motto of the **House of Siricus** sums up Pompeii's parvenu creed: *Salve Lucru* ('Hail Money!').

Pompeii's largest baths, the **Terme Stabianae** , occupy nearly a block at the end of this street, with the entrance on the broad Via dell'Abbondanza. To the

A tour of the baths

right of the portal is the men's section; beyond, in the women's baths, see the remains of the boiler room and the air space in the walls and floor where steam and hot air circulated.

THEATRES

Across the Via dell'Abbondanza to the right, follow the Via dei Teatri to the **Triangular Forum**, one of the city's earliest sacred precincts, to two theatres. A gateway leads into the forum, flanked by a long row of columns and shaded by old ilex and cypress trees. It is a quiet and restful spot, especially welcome on a hot day. At the rear, from the base of a 6th-century BC Doric temple, there is a good view across the Sarno River's clogged stream to modern Pompeii, Monte Faito and the Lattari range of the Sorrento peninsula.

The **Teatro Grande** ⓗ could seat 5,000 people, and is still used today for concerts and other performances. The adjoining

Teatro Piccolo or Odeion was originally roofed as a concert hall. A plaque reminded theatregoers that 'Claudio C.F. Marcello, Patrono' helped pay for the theatre. Most of Pompeii's public buildings were erected at the expense of rich citizens, who were often vote-seeking politicians. Beyond the large theatre is a colonnaded exercise field and the **Casa dei Gladiatori** ❶ (House of the Gladiators). Sixty-four bodies were found inside, some in chains, along with a rich store of weapons and armour, now housed in the Museo Archeologico Nazionale. The House of Gladiators famously collapsed in 2010 after a night of heavy rainfall and restoration work only got underway in late 2015.

COMMERCIAL POMPEII

Returning by the Via Stabiana to the Via dell'Abbondanza, turn right and follow it into the area of the **Nuovi Scavi**, the 'new' excavations begun in 1911. This is a district of small industries, shops, taverns, hotels and the villas of a few wealthy businessmen. An effort has been made to reconstruct these premises and to leave some of their contents in place, including casts of bodies found here. Most Pompeiian houses were two-storeyed, but the upper floors were crushed by the weight of ash. Here, many have been restored. Look for fine mosaic floors, stucco and painted wall decorations, and the trappings of artisans and shopkeepers.

In a laundry, the **Fullonica Stephani** at No. 7 on the south side of Insula VI, vats for washing, dyeing and bleaching occupy the rear. A press stands to the left of the entry, where clothes were handed in through a window in the door. The upper floor held lodgings. Across the way, note the depth of ash-filled buildings still unexcavated. Around the corner to the right on this block are the House of the Underground Portico, where many bodies were found in the wine cellar; and the elegant **Casa di Menandro** ❿ (House of Menander). A collection of exquisite silverware, now in the Naples museum, was unearthed here. In the rear there is a chariot and the skeleton of a horse.

On the north side of the Via dell'Abbondanza, the **Thermopolium of Asellina** is a very well-preserved bar. Note the graffiti advertising the names and attractions of prostitutes available in the upstairs beds. At the end of the street, the **Villa di Giulia Felice** (Villa of Julia Felix) takes up most of the block. It was apparently a hotel, for there are 'rooms to let' signs on the walls. It had its own baths, a garden and shops.

Behind the villa is the **Anfiteatro** (Amphitheatre), the oldest surviving in Italy. Seating just 20,000, it was small by Italian standards. To the west, the nearby **Grande Palestra** is a vast exercise field 100m square, enclosed on three sides by a covered portico and pine and plane trees. Roots of the original trees were found, and the planting has been recreated.

CAPRI

The breathtaking beauty of **Capri** lives up to its reputation. Two sheer bluffs of rock are joined in the middle by a lower, sloping saddle where white buildings cluster and spill down towards a busy, picturesque harbour.

This is the **Marina Grande**, where ferries laden with day-trippers constantly come and go amid much

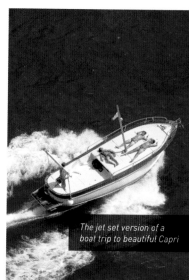

The jet set version of a boat trip to beautiful Capri

flinging of ropes and shouting on the dock. A small visitor's centre can be found at the end of the quay. You can take an open-top taxi or bus to the island's epicentre, the tiny Piazza Umberto I, better known as the **Piazzetta**. However, the best way to reach Capri Town's main square is to take the funicular (departures every 15 minutes). The cable-car climbs the steep slope past lemon groves and flower-filled gardens, and delivers you to the terrace of **Capri Town Ⓐ**. The views from here are spectacular. To the left (west),

Ⓞ EVERYONE'S FAVOURITE ISLAND

Over the centuries, Capri has been coveted and claimed by numerous powers and their leaders. Augustus Caesar traded Ischia to the Neapolitans for it in 29BC. His successor, Tiberius, withdrew to Capri in AD26 when he was 67. He built the Villa Jovis and several other palaces and spent the last 11 years of his life on the island. During the Middle Ages Capri changed hands according to the chequered fortunes of Naples, and was repeatedly raided by pirates right into the late 1700s. The British occupied it from 1806 to 1808 during the Napoleonic Wars. The island finally came into its own with 19th-century Romanticism; after the Blue Grotto was 'discovered' in 1827, it became an obligatory stop on the Grand Tour. In 1906 Maxim Gorky created a school of revolution here and brought over Lenin as a director. In the next decades the success of Norman Douglas's *South Wind* and of *The Story of San Michele* by the Swedish doctor Axel Munthe spread the island's fame as a retreat of artists and eccentrics. Both the Germans and the Allies used it as a rest camp during World War II. After the war the international jet set moved in and, despite an increasing flood of tourists and day trippers, still claims Capri as its own.

Anacapri is perched on the massive grey limestone block of Monte Solaro, the island's highest point; to the right is Monte (or Salto di) Tiberio, the perch from which Tiberius ruled the Roman Empire. Below is the harbour and straight ahead across the bay are Vesuvius and the crags and cliffs of the Sorrentine peninsula.

Santo Stefano overlooks Capri's heart, the Piazzetta

CAPRI TOWN

If the terrace is Capri's balcony, the Piazzetta is its salon. The intimate little square is enclosed on three sides by cafés, bars and shops, and on the fourth by steps to the small 17th-century church of Santo Stefano. The Piazzetta is filled with umbrella-shaded tables and is most enjoyable in the evening when the day trippers have caught the last hydrofoil out and the area is frequented by those fortunate enough to inhabit the island's myriad villas. There are no cars in the town proper – the lanes and alleys are far too narrow – but small electric tractors can get through to carry provisions to shops and hotels, as well as luggage. Taxis and buses stop some 50m (55yds) short of the Piazzetta, and a tiny visitor's centre at the base of the clock tower is available to answer any question in any language.

From the Piazzetta, take Via V. Emanuele, with its designer boutiques, past the legendary Hotel Quisisana (www.quisisana.com) and turn left to the **Certosa di San Giacomo** (www.coopculture.it; Tue–Sun Nov–Apr 10am–3pm,May until 6pm, Jun–Aug until 7pm,

Capri's coastline

Sep–Oct until 5pm), a 14th-century Carthusian monastery which houses a school and a museum of paintings from the 17th to the 19th centuries. The view from the monastery gardens encompasses the dramatic **Faraglioni** (a trio of rocks that rise 105m/345ft out of the sea) below and Monte Solaro above. An equally breathtaking panorama can be seen from the terraced gardens of the nearby **Giardini di Augusto** (www.coopculture.it; daily Apr–Oct 9am–7.30pm, Nov–Mar 9.30am–5.30pm), a little way along on Via Matteotti. Inside the shady gardens stands a memorial to Lenin, a curious intrusion into this playground of capitalism.

From the belvedere, you can see two higher lookout points – the **Punta del Cannone** and the **Castiglione** belvederes can both be reached along the Via Madre Serafina, which starts behind the Santo Stefano church.

From the Parco Augusto, **Via Krupp** descends in dizzying corkscrew turns down to the **Marina Piccola ❸**. The path is technically *chiuso* (closed) because of the danger of falling rocks, but this does not deter Capri regulars from using it. The Marina Piccola is their favourite bathing beach and watering hole. From the little strand you can rent a boat or kayak or join a cruise along the dramatic indented coast. Taxis linger here and buses run back up to town every 20 minutes.

COASTAL STROLLS

A very enjoyable walk, where you can enjoy a closer look at the Faraglioni, takes you from the Hotel Quisisana along the boutique-lined Via Camerelle to the **Punta Tragara.** If you're up to a modest hike of about an hour (along mostly shaded walkways), keep going along the coast path to the **Arco Naturale**. On the way you'll see the curious modern red house that the eminent Italian writer Curzio Malaparte had built in the late 1930s suspended over the sea. You'll pass a deep cave, the **Grotta di Matermania**, with some remains of a Roman sanctuary, and then climb steps up through pines to a natural limestone arch that frames a fine shot for photographers.

From the Piazzetta you can take either Via Longano or Via Le Botteghe to visit Tiberius's **Villa Jovis C** (www.coopculture.it; daily 9am–1hr before sunset). It is a relatively hard 45-minute climb to the park at 335m (1,095ft). The villa was one of 12 Imperial palaces built on the island by Emperor Tiberius, who ruled the Roman Empire from Capri for 10 years.

Long ago looted of everything interesting, the site itself is not that exciting, but the **views** from here are breathtaking. The whole island is at your feet. Punta Campanella, on the tip of the Sorrento headland, is only 5km (3 miles) across the water. From this eagle's nest the reclusive, ageing Tiberius ruled the Western world and, according to Roman biographers, indulged in monstrous orgies. On the highest point is the infamous Salto di Tiberio (Tiberius' Leap), from where the sadistic emperor hurled his enemies and unsatisfactory lovers.

ANACAPRI

The island's only other town, **Anacapri D** has relatively little of the glamour of Capri. There is a quiet backwater charm in its meandering, tree-shaded streets, owing to its relative remoteness and high altitude (283m/930ft). Noise and bustle are confined to the lane leading to Anacapri's tourist mecca, the tranquil, cool **Villa San Michele** (http://villasanmichele.eu; May–Sept 9am–6pm; Apr and Oct 9am–5pm; Nov–Feb 9am–3.30pm; Mar 9am–4.30pm). In stark contrast, the once peaceful path up to the villa is now a garish bazaar, selling local perfume and liqueurs, T-shirts and the gamut of kitsch knick-knacks.

Nestled against the steep hillside, the Villa was built in 1896 on the site of an ancient Roman manor. It contains Axel Munthe's collection of Roman sculpture (both authentic and fake), antique furniture and prints. From the outside terraces there are breathtaking views of Monte Tiberio and the bay.

Retracing your steps to the village square, you'll find the entrance to the chairlift (*seggiovia*; www.capriseggiovia.it; daily May–Oct 9.30am–5pm, Nov–Feb 9.30am–3.30pm, Mar–Apr 9.30am–4pm) to **Monte Solaro**, at 589m (1,926ft) the highest point on the island. The chair rides over vineyards and pines to the peak and a 360-degree panorama of the island, Ischia, the Campanian coast, and the distant Appenine Mountains. A delightful trail through golden broom descends past the solitary and picturesque 14th-century Santa Maria Cetrella chapel on the lip of the precipice and back to Anacapri in 40 minutes.

Off the beaten track, down Via Orlandi to the Piazza San Nicola, is **San Michele Church** (www.chiesa-san-michele.com; daily Apr–Sept 9am–7pm; Oct–Mar 10am–3pm), worth seeing for its beautiful floor, a naive Garden of Eden scene done in majolica tiles by an 18th-century artist.

THE BLUE GROTTO

From Anacapri the island's eastern side drops to low cliffs and coves reached by two roads, each served by a regular bus service. The bus marked 'Faro' goes to the lighthouse at Punta

The magical Blue Grotto

Carena, the island's wildest and least visited corner. This is a good swimming cove with a restaurant.

The other bus goes to a landing-stage next to Capri's most celebrated attraction, the **Grotta Azzurra** Ⓔ or **Blue Grotto** (www.coopculture.it; Apr–Oct 7.30am–6pm, Nov–Mar 8.30am–2pm), which you can also reach on organised tours, usually by boat from the Marina Grande.

When a wonder of the world becomes as famous as Capri's Blue Grotto, high expectations risk disappointment. Not so with this magical cavern and its glowing electric blue and silver waters: the Blue Grotto lives up to the rhapsodies it has inspired since it was 'discovered' in 1827.

The entrance to the Blue Grotto is an opening barely wide and high enough for a rowing boat, with passengers having to duck. Sunlight filtered from above through this opening irradiates the water with an ethereal blue that flashes and sparkles silver when a hand or oars are trailed below the surface. The best time for viewing is around midday. A flotilla of rowing boats constantly comes and goes through the tunnel to the accompaniment of shouts from boatmen and squeals of delight from tourists. The price of fame is overcrowding: it is unusual (but not impossible) to be one of a privileged few enjoying the grotto's beauty.

ISCHIA AND PROCIDA

Ischia ㉕ is the largest and most diverse of the islands in the Bay of Naples, though a bus ride around its serpentine roads takes less than two hours passing through or near its six principal towns. It has a life of its own beyond tourism (though it swells to six times its population in summer months), mainly based on the production of a delightful light white wine (so famous in antiquity that Ischia was known to the Romans as Aenaria – wine-land), as well as a thriving fishing industry and the cultivation of chestnuts and lemons.

The volcanic island is a mass of green vines, orchards and pines, rising to the central peak of Monte Epomeo. Ischia's volcano is extinct, but it continues to steam away like a leaky boiler and underground activity is ubiquitous. As you travel around the island, you'll see puffs of white issuing from pipes in the back gardens of homes and cracks in the hillsides.

As well as yielding excellent wine, the volcanic terrain produces bubbling hot springs prized for their therapeutic powers since Roman times. Ischia has 70 hot springs and 100 thermal bath establishments. Italians and Germans who come here on a regular basis swear by them for the effective treatment of rheumatism, arthritis, circulatory disorders, sciatica, even obesity and premature ageing. But you don't have to be suffering from an ailment to benefit. There is nothing more therapeutic for the weary traveller than a day spent wallowing in hot springs and thermal pools, maybe indulging in a mud bath, massage or facial treatment.

A CIRCULAR TOUR OF ISCHIA

In 1301 an eruption buried the principal town under a flow of lava that today is a pine grove and park sepa-

A causeway connects Ischia Ponte to the Castello Aragonese

rating **Ischia Porto** from the older town of **Ischia Ponte**, a 20-minute walk to the east. Ischia Porto is the main gateway to the island. To the right of the ferry dock an information office dispenses maps and booklets. Behind it is the parking space for buses that go round the island in both directions. If you want to do the driving yourself, the island is very easy to navigate and there are a number of car hire companies operating in the area (the tourist office will supply you with a list).

Ischia's most famous landmark, the **Castello Aragonese** (www.castelloaragoneseischia.com; daily 9am–until sunset), caps a steep-sided fortified islet linked to Ischia Ponte by a causeway. The castle is privately owned, but you can visit the ruins and take an elevator to the top, where a small hotel occupies part of the former Convent of Poor Clares. On an adjoining terrace you will find the entrance to the cemetery of the nuns. This is a chamber where the dead were seated against

The black volcanic sand of Ischia's beaches

the walls and left to mummify. Further on are the cells where from 1851 to 1860 the Bourbon rulers of Naples imprisoned Italian nationalist patriots.

Continuing around the island clockwise, the road from Ponte climbs past vineyards and farms with storehouses carved out of the soft sandstone. From **Serrara Fontana**, it takes about an hour on foot to reach the closest point to the peak of **Monte Epomeo**, and not much less by the guided mules you can rent here. From the 760m (2,500ft) summit, another hour's hike will bring you down to towns on the other side of the island.

As the road descends abruptly, passing Serrara, you get a good view towards Capri before the bus turns off at Panza for **Sant'Angelo G**. This popular little seaside village has numerous restaurants around its promontory, La Roia, and the cafés and shops that make it a charming destination. Several hotels with thermal baths are perched on the mountainside just above the **Lido dei Maronti**, Ischia's longest and broadest volcanic black-sand beach. Steam hisses from fumaroles in the sand, and in nearby ravines are steamy caves and do-it-yourself mud baths used since antiquity.

As you approach **Forio H**, you will notice more and more signs in German. Since the 1980s, Ischia has been a favourite resort of German tourists, and Forio is their capital. The cafés on the village square and waterfront are lively international crossroads. Just out of town are the **Poseidon Gardens** (www.giardiniposeidon.it), a series of 22 outdoor thermal pools near the beach that are one of the island's most popular attractions. Forio is also the centre of wine production, and wineries often invite visitors to sample their Epomeo vintages. The gleaming white church on the headland above the harbour is the **Santuario del Soccorso**. Inside it is filled with votive offerings for the protection of fishermen and sailors.

Just outside Forio is **La Mortella** (Apr–Oct Tue, Thu, Sat–Sun 9am–7pm; www.lamortella.org), the estate of English composer Sir William Walton (1902–83), famous for the gardens planted with over 1,000 exotic species. They were laid out by the landscape architect Russell Page and lovingly cultivated over 40 years by Walton's green-fingered wife, Lady Susana until she passed away in 2010. Afternoon concerts given by young musicians sponsored by the William Walton Trust are held at weekends in spring and autumn, and on Thursdays in summer.

At the island's western end is the picturesque cup-shaped harbour of **Lacco Ameno**. Every year on 17 May, the town explodes in an eruption of fireworks to celebrate the island's patron saint, Santa Restituta. Lacco Ameno's elegant spas make the unique boast of offering the most radioactive water and mud treatments in Italy.

Next comes **Casamicciola Terme ❶**, a long stretch of thermal pools and hotels along the coast. The alkaline Gurgitello spring spouts 68ºC (154ºF) water and steam, in which devotees cook themselves in boxes with just their heads sticking out of the top. Henrik Ibsen, who worked on *Peer Gynt* here in 1867, would not recognise the place. Casamicciola was completely rebuilt after an earthquake in 1883, which took 3,000 lives. The town straggles towards Porto d'Ischia, completing the circuit.

PROCIDA

Procida ㉖ is the smallest and least touristic of the island trio. That is not to say that tourism doesn't play an important role. In the summer months, the island's population is doubled by day-trippers from the mainland. They bring good business to the shops, hotels and restaurants, but not at the expense of the fishing and farming communities, which are still integral to the island's economy. Fishing is in the Procidan blood, while the rich volcanic soil is ideal for the cultivation of vineyards and citrus groves (Procida's lemons are reputedly the tangiest in Italy). The island covers only 4 sq km (1.5 sq miles) and you can easily walk round it in a day – or, as this itinerary suggests, walk round half of it, loll on a beach after lunch, then catch a bus back to the port.

Ferries and hydrofoils dock at **Marina Grande**, a colourful jumble of boats and sun-baked houses. As you come off the boat, turn left and meander along the harbour, past the restaurants, bars, fishmongers and shops to the **Chiesa Santa Maria della Pietà** (1760). With your back to the white church, take Via Vittorio Emanuele and walk uphill past the tourist office to Piazza dei Martiri and the yellow clifftop church of **Santa Maria delle Grazie**. It is a short climb from here to the **Abbazia San Michele Arcangelo** ❶ (www.abbaziasan micheleprocida.it; Mon–Sat 10am–12.45pm, 10am–12.45pm and 3–5pm; church free, museum charge). The whitewashed domes of the abbey church rise above Terra Murata, the ruins of a citadel built to defend the island from Saracen attack. The three-naved church features a wooden coffered ceiling

Procida still retains its fishing and farming communities

decorated with fine gold and a central painting of the arch-
angel Michael by Luca Giordano (1699). There is also a small
museum and a set of catacombs.

On your way back down to Piazza dei Martiri, stop at the
terrace of the abandoned Castello and admire views of the
ruined citadel above and **Corricella** below. This enchanting
fishing village can be reached via a flight of steps from the
piazza. Corricella is the most traditional village on the island,
a warren of pastel-painted houses built into a sheltered cove,
inter-connected by arches and stone stairways giving it a dis-
tinct Moorish feel.

Another set of steps at the far end of Corricella takes you
back up to the main road. Turn left into Via Scotti, which
becomes Via Vittorio Emanuele. Turn left again into the much
quieter Via Pizzaco, which commands lovely views across the
bay to the abbey and Corricella.

At the second fork in the road, veer right into Via Mozzo and continue hugging the coast, enjoying views of Capo Miseno on the mainland, until you reach Via Solchiaro. Turn left then right into Via S. Schiano, which leads to **Marina Chiaiolella**, a berth for yachts and small boats. From here you can see **Isola di Vivara**, a tiny volcanic island joined to Procida by a footbridge. Once a hunting ground for the Bourbon kings, Vivara is now a nature reserve and bird sanctuary (www.isolavivara.it; guided tours by appointment).

The stretch of sand on the marina's western side is Procida's longest and most popular beach (strictly two beaches: **Ciracciello** and **Ciraccio**). Stake out a patch of sand and enjoy a swim and siesta. A bus runs back to the port from here.

SORRENTO AND ITS PENINSULA

Sorrento 27 is the *grande dame* of Neapolitan resorts, but there is very little sightseeing to do here. The most agreeable pastimes are strolling along lanes where flowering vines spill over garden walls, or walking down shady paths by the cliff edge, stopping for refreshment at a terrace bar or café perched above the bay. These days the town is above all a base for exploring the Sorrentine peninsula, the islands and the Amalfi Coast. Bus tours are what keep this formerly elitist resort town in business, and tourism is still its game.

Hydrofoils and ferries from Naples or Capri dock at the

Intarsia

Intarsia – detailed and delicate wood inlay – is the craft most associated with Sorrento, and *intarsia* workshops can still be found in the upper part of the town. Once ubiquitous, the intricate and expensive work now takes some tracking down.

Marina Piccola where jostling hotel porters and tour guides await. The winding road from the harbour leads to Sorrento's main square, the **Piazza Tasso,** named after Sorrento's favourite son, the Renaissance poet Torquato Tasso (1544–95). If you arrive by car or by train, you will reach the Piazza Tasso via the **Corso d'Italia**, Sorrento's central thoroughfare.

Sedile Dominova, on the square Largo Dominova

Sorrento's landmarks can be visited in short walks from this main square. The tourist office (www.sorrento tourism.com; also known as the Circolo dei Forestieri) on Via L. de Maio just off the square, will supply you with a map of the town. Heading west from the square, Corso Italia leads to the **Duomo** (www.cattedralesorrento.it; daily 8am–12.30pm, 4.30–9pm; free) Sorrento's cathedral. Although much altered over the centuries, it has noteworthy inlaid wood stalls in the choir; the intarsia work is still done by Sorrentine craftsmen.

Cross the Corso and wander into the heart of the old centre of Sorrento; its street plan dates back to Greek and Roman times. The skinny Via Cesareo is lined with souvenir shops selling bright ceramics, inlaid boxes and trinkets, bottles of limoncello, the sweet and sticky local liqueur, and a whole host of knick-knacks decorated or scented with lemons. On the corner of Via Giuliani is the **Sedile Dominova**, a 16th-century loggia that was the summer meeting place for Sorrentine aristocrats.

Find sunloungers, cafés and tour boats at Marina Piccola

Today, it is the domain of old men who sit around tables under the majolica dome playing cards and talking politics.

From here, pick your way through the narrow streets to Villa Comunale, a shady park at the cliff edge with wonderful views over the Bay of Naples. Sorrento's grand and formerly grand hotels (Tramontano, Excelsior, Bellevue, etc.) are ranged along the clifftop. At the edge of the park stands the Baroque church of **San Francesco**, with its onion-dome belltower.

From the terrace of the park, you can take the steps or lift down to the beach platforms of **Marina Piccola**. Sorrento is not known for its beaches, but if your hotel is lacking a pool, you can come down to one of the handful of public *stabilimenti* and hire a parasol and sun lounger for a small fee.

The Via Veneto leads from the Villa Comunale to the Piazza Vittoria. From here, follow Via Marina Grande down through the old Greek gateway to the harbour. Confusingly called

Marina Grande, the 'Big Port', it is in fact the smaller and more down at heel of the two, but is all the more charming for it. This is one of the most authentic corners of Sorrento and an ideal dinner location.

Returning to the Piazza Tasso, cross the ravine and follow the Via Correale east past parks and hotels to the **Museo Correale di Terranova** (www.museocorreale.it; Tue–Sat 9.30am–6.30pm, Sun 9.30am–1.30pm), the only real point of cultural interest in town. The 18th-century villa (with lovely gardens) now houses a museum whose offerings include an excellent collection of 17th-century Neapolitan paintings, inlaid intarsia furniture and Capodimonte porcelain of the region.

EXPLORING THE PENINSULA

The road from Sorrento to the tip of the peninsula begins with the Corso as it leads out of town towards Massa Lubrense. Soon after leaving Sorrento, a turning to the right, marked by a sign, leads down a very narrow lane through fields and olive groves to the ruins of the Roman **Villa of Pollio Felix**, on a superb site at the tip of a small cape. Boatmen from Sorrento can take you to this pretty picnic spot, where there is good swimming off the rocks.

There is swimming, too, on the small stony beaches and coves out on the cape, some accessible only by the boats available for rent at fishing villages such as Marina di Puolo and Marina della Lobra, the little harbour below Massa Lubrense. It is a great area for snorkelling.

Termini is the departure point for one of the loveliest walks on the peninsula. Park outside the yellow church, stock up on water and a snack from the bar, then follow the signs to the 'Punto Panoramico' to reach **Punta Campanella**. The road soon gives way to a footpath that descends slowly through terraced lemon and olive groves, past a Saracen watchtower, to the tip of the peninsula. The views from here are breathtaking and Capri is so close you could almost reach out and touch it. The uphill return is more strenuous. Allow about two hours in total.

Just beyond Termini, the road to Nerano winds down steeply to the popular **Marina del Cantone** beach on the Gulf of Salerno. Small hotels, *pensioni* and apartments in villages atop the peninsula's ridge are inexpensive bases for exploring the coast and enjoying the spectacular views on foot, by bus or by car.

The best panoramic view is from the medieval convent **Il Deserto** ㉘ (call in advance to arrange access, tel:081-878 0199, or try ringing the bell), on a terraced hill above the village of **Sant'Agata sui due Golfi** (396m/1,300ft above sea level and always favoured for its vistas). It takes in the whole region, from Capri to Ischia and Cape Miseno.

The road back to Sorrento from Sant'Agata is the 'Nastro Azzurro' (Blue Ribbon), the first stretch of the scenic route to Positano and the Amalfi coast.

THE AMALFI COAST

One of the most beautiful excursions in the world, the fabled Amalfi Coast drive consists of one astonishing view after another, but you won't see much of them if you are behind the wheel. The road is a veritable marvel of engineering – a narrow, serpentine ribbon cut out of the rock, clinging to the contours of mountains that drop steeply into the sea. Drivers worry about dropping into the sea, too, as they navigate curves with the mountain wall on one side, only a low barrier on the other, and huge tour buses bearing down ahead. Timid drivers should seriously consider travelling by private taxi or taking public transport. Parking is yet another nightmare.

Suspended between sea and sky for most of its 45km (28 miles), the drive links a string of cliff-hanging towns and coastal communities that were once the territory of Amalfi, the oldest maritime republic in Italy.

POSITANO

Coming from Sorrento, the first (and the coastline's most fashionable) stop is **Positano** ㉙, a jumble of pastel-hued, cube-shaped houses that spill in ter-

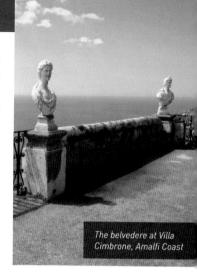

The belvedere at Villa Cimbrone, Amalfi Coast

races down the flanks of a ravine. There is nothing close to level in Positano except the beach, the semi-sandy **Spiaggia Grande**. Instead of streets, the town has a network of steep steps. Fortunately, a bus (6am–8pm; www.positano.com) makes a regular circuit from the Amalfi drive along Positano's only road and back, coming fairly close to most hotels and connecting Positano with neighbouring coastal towns. There are a few parking garages that offer only limited hope of available space.

The road does not penetrate the oldest part of Positano and the beach area, still only reachable on foot through a maze of whitewashed alleys. The principal one, **Via dei Mulini**, passes the inviting courtyard of the 18th-century **Palazzo Murat**, (now a gracious hotel; see page 138) where summer concerts are held. The pathway is lined with racks of resort fashions, the wares of sandal-makers and galleries of every description. Positano was once known for its casual resortwear, a look

Praiano enjoys a spectacular setting

that outgrew its appeal some decades ago. It has discreetly up-market hotels, yachts riding just offshore, casual but good restaurants, and bougainvillaea-draped villas belonging to an international roster of the rich and famous. At the height of the summer season the grey sands of the Spiaggia Grande disappear under rows of reclining chairs and ranks of beached boats for hire, and it's hard to find a table on the arboured terraces of the popular seafront restaurants.

A lane along the cliff to the right (west) of the Spiaggia Grande (and the concrete **Marina Grande** pier there) winds past a round watchtower and leads to **Fornillo Beach**, also commandeered by beach-chair renters. A number of idyllic uncrowded coves are nearby, reached by hiring a rowing boat or being taken out by a private service (see agency booths set up on shore for these short excursions). Boat trips further afield are popular, to fishing villages up and down the coast and out to the three private isles **I Galli**, once owned by the ballet star Rudolf Nureyev and now in the hands of a European corsortium.

After Positano the drive reaches **Praiano** ㉚, a village scattered along the Capo Sottile headland. Less sophisticated (and crowded) than Positano, it nevertheless accommodates some of Positano's overflow. At the Saracen defence tower, steps descend to Marina di Praia's beach, where boats can be hired.

It is impossible to compare the views along this coast – each more magnificent than the last. Ancient footpaths lead to small, secluded coves where you can swim off the rocks. The next headland is **Conca dei Marini** ('Seafarers' Basin'), with a large parking space for the lift down to the **Grotta dello Smeraldo** ㉛, the Emerald Grotto (daily 9am–4pm). This large illuminated cavern's water is a brilliant gem-like green and is a popular sight. A landslide breached the cave, letting in the sea and covering stalagmites and stalactites reflected in the emerald depths. But the hassle of high-season crowds may discourage all but dedicated grotto fanatics.

AMALFI

As the road approaches **Amalfi** ㉜, 18km (11 miles) southeast of Positano, it passes tiny terraces cut into the cliffs where lemons, olives and vines are grown in soil laboriously carried up in baskets over the centuries. After a tunnel, Amalfi appears – all white houses with red tile roofs, joined together in what seems a single construction. The buses that line the seafront promenade testify that tourism is the main industry, but in its 11th- and 12th-century heyday Amalfi rivalled Pisa and Genoa as a mighty maritime power in the Mediterranean, when its population swelled to more than 100,000.

Nowhere is Amalfi's architecture more visibly influenced by its maritime dealings with the Arab world and points East than

Amalfi's Moorish-Arabesque Duomo

in its showpiece **Duomo di Sant'Andrea** (daily Mar–Jun 9am–6.45pm, Jul–Sep until 7.45pm, Nov–Feb 10am–1pm and 2.30–4.30pm). It is Amalfi's focal point, sitting atop a monumental 62-step staircase that confirmed the town's importance. Founded in the 9th century, this cathedral dedicated to St Andrew was remodelled several times, principally in the 13th century, yet retains its Moorish-Arabesque character. Its small cloister, the evocative location of summer concerts, is one of southern Italy's loveliest.

The compact town is divided between **Piazza del Duomo** and the store-lined Via Genova, and the bustling waterfront **Piazza Flavio Gioia** (named for the Amalfi-born inventor of the compass), made up of a bus and car park and the pier where boats depart for the islands, Naples and Positano. By the piazza is the **Antico Arsenale della Repubblica** (Largo Cesareo Console 3; Mar–Sep daily 10am–8pm, Oct–Feb Tue–Sun 10am–1.30pm, 3.30–7pm), old shipyards converted into a showcase of modern art featuring Andy Warhol and Giorgio di Chirico. Also here is the **Museo della Bussola e del Ducato Marinaro di Amalfi**, dedicated to Amalfi's heyday as a maritime republic.

Meander around town and you will stumble upon the narrowest possible staircase alleys, or *salitas*, that climb the hills. One such byway, above the Duomo's Cloister of Paradise, leads to the tiny 10th-century **Santa Maria Maggiore**.

Continuing 15 or 20 minutes up the main Via Genova you can soon hear the river gurgling underfoot. It emerges where the outskirts of Amalfi become the **Valle dei Mulini**, Valley of the Mills. Now in ruins, these were the first paper mills in Europe. The Amalfitani learned the process from the Arabs, who had picked it up from the Chinese. There is a walk along the valley of the mills and the **Museo Della Carta** (Paper Museum, Valle dei Mulini 23; www.museodellacarta.it; Mar–Oct daily 10am–6.30pm, Nov–Jan Tue–Sun until 4pm; closed Feb) shows you the handmade paper-making process and sells you the products.

RAVELLO

The road from Atrani, just past Amalfi, twists up the dark, narrow Dragone Gorge to **Ravello** ㉝, a medieval relic pinned to a ridge 362m (1,184ft) above the sea. Of all the coast's spectacular views, Ravello's is considered by many to be the best. Seductive views are a modern notion, however; the merchant/founders of Ravello chose the site because it is naturally protected by cliffs on three sides, making it easy to defend against raiders.

Most of Ravello's lanes are too narrow for vehicles (drivers must leave their cars outside town), but perfect for leisurely rambles. The main square is dominated by the austere 11th-century **Duomo** (www.chiesaravello.com; church daily 9am–noon, 5.30–7pm, museum daily 9am–7pm, winter until 6pm; church free), the cathedral dedicated to patron saint San Pantaleone and founded in 1086.

Just beyond the piazza, in the superb **Villa Rufolo** gardens (www.villarufolo.it; summer daily 9am–8pm; winter daily 9am–sunset), huge pines and cypresses shade the shattered walls and towers of the 11th-century Rufolo castle. A festival of classical music is held here in the summer (www.ravellofestival.com). This is the inspirational spot of which Wagner wrote in 1880, 'This is Klingsor's garden,' the embodiment of his vision for the third act of *Parsifal*.

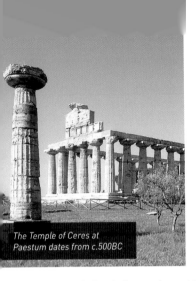

The Temple of Ceres at Paestum dates from c.500BC

A short walk from the monastery leads to Ravello's other enchanting gardens, the **Villa Cimbrone** (www.villacimbrone.com; summer daily 9am–8pm; winter daily 9am–sunset). This dramatic residence (now operating as a hotel; see page 140) and garden is the caprice of a 19th-century English owner who created it out of medieval bits and pieces. The romantic atmosphere is not lessened by a plaque recording that the 'divine Greta Garbo' stole 'hours of secret happiness' here with Leopold Stokowski in the spring of 1938. At the end of a tree-lined alley is a bust-lined clifftop belvedere on the very tip of Ravello's ridge, whose view over the entire Bay of Salerno, wrote local resident author Gore Vidal, was 'the most beautiful in the world'.

A scenic road from Ravello winds over the mountains to join the Naples–Salerno *autostrada* at Nocera. This alternative route makes it easy to visit Pompeii in a day trip from the coastal resorts.

PAESTUM

Three of the finest Greek temples in existence have survived remarkably intact for more than 2,500 years on an isolated coastal plain south of Salerno. Greek colonists founded Poseidonia (named after the sea-god Poseidon) in the 6th century BC. The Romans renamed it **Paestum** ㉞ in 273BC when they took over the settlement and enlarged it. After the fall of Rome, the city sank into a decline, and more or less vanished from the map and history until the 18th century, when Charles III, the indefatigable Bourbon builder, had a road constructed across the plain. Cutting through the underbrush, the labourers uncovered ruins and ran the road right across them, much as you find it today.

The most direct route from Naples to Paestum is to take the A3 *autostrada* for 73km (44 miles), exiting at Battipaglia and continuing another 20km (12.5 miles) to the ruins. The entrance to **Paestum** (www.museopaestum.beniculturali.it; daily 8.30am–until sunset) is near the southern end. Straight ahead of the entrance in a grassy field are Paestum's greatest temples, the **Temple of Poseidon** (or Neptune) and, to its left, the **Basilica** – both names having been incorrectly applied in the 18th century. It was later proved that both temples were dedicated to Hera, wife of Zeus.

The Basilica is Paestum's earliest construction, guessed to be around 565BC, pre-dating the Parthenon of Athens by nearly a century. Its somewhat heavy and bulging fluted columns and the flattened discs of the Doric capitals mark it as archaic, when the Doric style was evolving. The Temple of Poseidon was built about 100 years later on the pattern of the Temple of Zeus at Olympia, its 36 fluted Doric columns making it one of Magna Graecia's finest.

Behind these temples a paved Roman road runs alongside an area that held the city's principal public buildings and passes the third temple. This dignified structure, known as the **Temple of Ceres**, was actually dedicated to Athena.

Unique antiques

The Paestum museum (8.30am–7.30pm, 1st and 3rd Mon until 1.40pm) has a collection of terracotta pots, fragments of Doric friezes and tomb murals – the only ancient Greek paintings to survive anywhere.

Positano's semi-sandy beach

WHAT TO DO

SPORTS

There are sports facilities in Naples and throughout the coastal resort region, both for those who like to participate and for spectators. If you want to play **tennis**, the courts of the Tennis Club Napoli (www.tennisclubnapoli.it) are in the Villa Comunale, at the Piazza della Vittoria end, and on the Vomero on Via Rossini. Have your hotel call to book a court, especially in resort towns. If you prefer **golf**, there is a nine-hole course in Pozzuoli, just outside Naples (www.golfnapoli.it).

You have to go well beyond the Naples harbour to find safe **swimming**. The nearest clean-water beaches are at Posillipo, west of the town, although they tend to be overrun in high season. Clean water can also be found a little further at Cape Miseno, where numerous bathing beaches can be reached by the Cumana rail line. Far more enticing are the beaches of the islands, Sorrentine peninsula and Amalfi Coast. Capri and Ischia are stony shingle; swimming is mainly done off the rocks. The same is true for Sorrento's bathing platforms beneath the cliff, while visitors to Amalfi and elsewhere often ferret out idyllic little coves. **Snorkelling** equipment is available to hire on Positano's beach, and many resorts offer **windsurfing** and **sailing**.

Despite the Mediterranean's depleted fish stocks, it is still possible to go **fishing** for tuna and swordfish in boats from the small ports of the Sorrento peninsula. A line and a rod are all you need to join those angling from the rocks beyond Naples' Santa Lucia, but the waters here are far from pristine.

Hikers can find lovely walks in the hills on Sorrento's cape, in the Monti Lattari backing the Amalfi Coast and around the Phlegraean

Fields. There are also gentle climbs up Monte Epomeo on Ischia, up Monte Faito from Castellamare di Stabia, and in numerous locations across Capri. For organised excursions, Giovanni Visetti (tel: 339-694 2911) is a friendly and knowledgeable local guide; his website (www.giovis.com), is an excellent resource.

For spectators, **horse racing** is a year-round spectacle and race goers should head to the Ippodromo di Agnano (www. ippodromoagnano.it), a few kilometres from the stadium off the *tangenziale*.

The Napoli **football** club (www.sscnapoli.it), one of Italy's most historic, was founded in 1904 as the Naples Football and Cricket Club, and is in Serie A. The exuberant enthusiasm of its many fans remains hard to beat. The 60,000-seat San Paolo stadium is in Fuorigrotta.

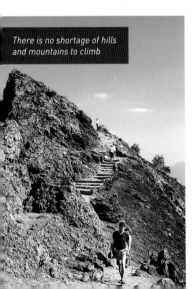

There is no shortage of hills and mountains to climb

SHOPPING

In general, shops open Mon–Sat 9am–1pm and 4–7pm or 8pm, although the big ones now stay open even on Sundays. During the summer, shops in resort towns close only when the last tourists leave the streets. In winter, many shops, even in Naples itself, simply shut for the season.

Look for **antiques** off Piazza della Vittoria, in the Vias Arcoleo and Gaetani, behind the Riviera di Chiaia, and in Via Santa Maria di Constantinopoli near the National Museum. Old chests, mirrors, engravings, porcelain and candlesticks might have come from a nearby palazzo. Alternatively, browse around the open-air flea market in the Villa Comunale (third Sunday of the month and preceding Saturday) for junk and gems.

High fashion and famous labels cluster around Piazza dei Martiri and Via Chiaia. Shoes can be purchased on Via Toledo, some of which are made in the cottage-industry factories in the back streets of Naples. While Capri is designer heaven, Ischia, Positano and Sorrento offer innumerable shops and stalls selling summer fashions, as well as handicrafts; sandals, straw hats and inexpensive handmade jewellery. There is a vast open-air second-hand clothes market at Resina (daily), adjoining Herculaneum. You will find first-rate garments at knock-down prices in a typically Neapolitan setting.

Ceramics of all kinds, whether shapes copied from Greek and Roman urns, jugs and plates, or depicting typical patterns of animals, fish and lemons, are the speciality of Vietri sul Mare and can be found all along the Amalfi Coast, particularly at Paestum.

The **figurines** of hand-painted terracotta made in Naples for Christmas cribs – called *presepi* – are an art handed down

Classic cameos

Cameos have been a Neapolitan art form since Roman times. In antiquity, white glass layered onto blue was carved to stand out in relief. Since the 19th century, seashells have replaced glass. Carvers scrape away the outer part of the shell to expose the white layer. The cameo design is painstakingly carved from the white material, often under a magnifying glass, leaving a background of chestnut-hued shell.

over the generations of families living around Via San Gregorio Armeno in the Spaccanapoli quarter of the old city. Here too there is a great difference in quality from plastic moulded run-of-the-mill shepherds and *pulcinella* figures to the justifiably expensive individual set pieces.

Cameos and **carved coral** are worked while you watch in the factory salesrooms of Torre del Greco, 13km (8 miles) from Naples, on the way to Vesuvius and Pompeii. Most tours to the historical sites include a stop at a cameo factory. Ask a shop-keeper to show you with a magnifying glass how to tell fine cameo carving from ordinary products.

Intarsia is the inlaid wood of different types and colors, made into objects such as boxes, trays, tables and frames in Sorrento. This, too, can be found elsewhere, but it is more

Coral jewellery in a Capri shop

fun seeing the delicate process carried out in a workshop and learning from the experts how to distinguish fine inlays from dyed and engraved designs.

Italian **housewares** are often handsomely designed, and can be found on Via Toledo in Naples. You might want to take back a 'Napoletana' pot for making espresso on your stove, or an electric steam *espresso* machine.

Comestibles of various kinds, such as good *vergine* olive oil, sun-dried tomatoes, a string of small bright red peppers or a rope of garlic, make good gifts. Find bottles of lemon and basil liqueurs in Capri and Sorrento, and interesting wines from Ischia and Ravello.

Records and **CDs** of old Neapolitan folksongs are sold in street markets, or try Feltrinelli (www.lafeltrinelli.it), Via Santa Caterina a Chiaia 23, in Naples.

ENTERTAINMENT

The greatest show in Naples, apart from the city itself, is surely opera in the Teatro San Carlo. Even if you are not fanatical about opera, don't miss the chance to see a performance in this landmark temple of *bel canto*; the hall itself is a gem. The season runs from January to mid-July and September to December (tel: 081-7972331; www.teatrosancarlo.it)

Concerts, from classical to rock, are part of the summer programmes of resort towns, while evening concerts and ballet are performed in the outdoor theatres of Pompeii, and in the 'Vesuvian Villas', restored palaces near Portici along the bay. Each resort has its own information office for details. To find out what is happening in Naples, check out *Qui Napoli*, a free monthly bulletin (with foreign translations of key information) distributed through most hotels and available to download from www.inaples.it. Another useful source of information is local website www.napoliunplugged.com which has events and sightseeing listings. The summer Ravello Festival (www.ravellofestival.com) is a two-month affair of orchestras, chamber groups, jazz performers, art shows and dance events.

The spirit of Naples and its surrounding communities is best evoked at the **street festivals** held in every district for a saint's day or other remembrance (see page 97). Many are in mid-summer, often involving fireworks and orgies of eating, which visitors can join in.

NIGHTLIFE

In the evenings, young people gather in their neighbourhood square, lingering outside caffès, lounging by their scooters and courting in the shadows. Naples nightlife is not exactly hectic. What Neapolitans like to do most in the evening is visit a cinema or theatre, then go on to a restaurant – in summer preferably one outdoors – for a long-drawn-out meal with friends and relatives, drink wine and listen to music. This isn't a bad recipe for the tourist, either. If you are lucky you may hear *O Marinariello* and *Santa Lucia* sung to a mandolin.

There are nightclubs and late-night bars on the bay, such as popular La Mela (40 Via dei Mille; tel: 081 251 2110) and the Bourbon Street Jazz And Spirits Bar (52 Via Vincenzo Bellini; www.bourbonstreetjazzclub.com), known for excellent live music. **Cammarota Spritz** (31 Vico Lungo Teatro Nuovo) is also an excellent place for an evening drink.

In Capri, the international jet-set flock to clubs such as **Anema & Core** (via Sella Orta 1; www.anemaecore.com/en) and **Panta Rei** (Via Lo Palazzo 1), while the top spot on the Amalfi Coast is Positano's Music on the Rocks (www.musicontherocks.it).

CALENDAR OF FESTIVALS

6 January *Naples* Epiphany: an old witch known as La Befana distributes presents to children on the Piazza del Plebiscito.

February *Carnevale:* The beginning of Lent is celebrated with parades. Children dress in carnival costumes; lasagne is the carnival dish.

19 March *Naples* Festa di San Giuseppe: special cakes known as *zeppole* are traditionally eaten.

Easter Good Friday processions all over the region, especially on Procida and in Sorrento and Massa Lubrense. The Monday after Easter, frenetic dancing known as *'Ndrezzata* ('intertwined') takes place at Buonopane on Ischia. Dancers wear traditional costumes and carry rolling pins.

May (first Saturday) *Naples:* Phials of San Gennaro's blood and his head in a silver reliquary are carried in procession from the Duomo to Santa Chiara, where the blood supposedly liquefies.

14 May *Capri:* A statue of the town's patron saint, San Costanzo, is carried in procession to the sea, where participants are blessed.

15 June *Positano:* Feast of the patron saint, San Vito.

24 June *Ischia:* Festival of San Giovanni Battista. More frantic *'Ndrezzata* dancing (see Easter Monday, above).

27 June *Amalfi:* Festival of Sant'Andrea. Costumes, fireworks, music and the blessing of the fishing fleet.

26 July *Ischia:* The patron saint, Sant'Anna, is honoured with a torchlight procession of hundreds of boats.

27 July *Ravello:* Feast of San Pantaleone celebrated with a spectacular firework display.

15 August *Ferragosto:* The Assumption is celebrated all over the region. Positano has a procession followed by fireworks.

19 September *Naples:* Feast of San Gennaro. The faithful gather in the Duomo to witness the liquefaction of the saint's blood.

Christmas *Naples:* Churches compete to build the finest *presepe* (nativity scene). Concerts held in city churches.

31 December *Naples:* New Year is ushered in with a concert and fireworks in the Piazza del Plebiscito.

EATING OUT

At its best, the food of southern Italy is essentially inspired home cooking, based on what's best that day in the market. You'll see housewives critically making their choices in the street markets of Old Naples – perfect plum tomatoes for sauce, big bunches of basil and flat-leaf parsley, fennel, artichokes, fat aubergines (eggplants), freshly picked chard, *bettola* greens, golden peppers, and hot, red *peperoncini*. There are also big onions and strings of garlic, lemons with their leaves on to prove freshness, and virgin olive oil. The greatest treats, now quite expensive, are fish and other seafood.

The cosmopolitan tide that floods the coastal resorts has brought many non-Neapolitan dishes to the menus of hotels and restaurants. There are elegant restaurants in Santa Lucia and Pizzofalcone, and more along the coast (see page 106 for Recommended Restaurants). But often a simple *trattoria*, with paper tablecloths and mamma at the stove, serves the most typical and satisfying fare. Dining alfresco in the shade of a vine arbour, or on a quay where fishing boats rock on the tide, or beside a wood-fired pizza oven that brings forth a sizzling *pizza margherita*, can be the high point of your day.

PASTA

Pasta is served as a first course, with meat or fish to follow. Eating pasta as often as twice a day, day after day, is considered essential to human well-being, and it's a notion that's difficult to contest.

Anything cooked *alla napoletana* will be bathed in a full-flavoured tomato *(pomodoro)* sauce. Made simply with lightly cooked fresh tomatoes, it has no peer. This blissful union of ingredients was some time coming, because, although pasta had been around

since Roman times (a half-eaten plate of *pasta e fagioli*, which is still served locally, was found in the ruins of Pompeii), the Neapolitans had to wait until the Spanish brought tomatoes back from Mexico in the 16th century before the recipe was complete.

Other favourite accompaniments include oil and garlic with parsley *(aglio e olio)*, clam sauce *(alle vongole)*, or chilli peppers *(alla siciliana)*. Besides *spaghetti* (from *spago*, meaning string), there are dozens of pasta shapes made in factories around Naples from firm durum wheat. *Rigatoni* and *ziti* are thick tubes, *farfalle* resemble butterflies, and *conchiglie* are shell-shaped. *Tagliolini* are very thin strands. *Fettuccine* are flat and often made with egg in the dough. *Tagliatelle* are from the same dough and flat, but cut as thin as *spaghetti*, while *lasagne* are very broad and are usually baked with their sauce.

The most popular type of pasta is *pasta asciutta*, made from a simple flour and water dough then dried. This is normally factory produced, whereas *pasta fresca* includes eggs for a softer dough and is made at home. Most restaurants usually carry one or two of the latter, changing daily.

PIZZA

The pizza of Naples has conquered the world, though the limp, soggy stuff often dished up abroad as fast food bears little resemblance to the real thing. Since the early 19th century Neapolitan pizzerias have been relaxed and friendly places where people can eat simply and cheaply. The secret of 'real' pizza is in the brick oven and the high temperature that makes the dough puffed and crunchy round the edges. That is why pizza is usually served only in the evening: not many eateries can crank up their ovens to maximum heat by lunchtime.

Pizza fresh from a brick oven

The *margherita* pizza is named after Queen Margherita, who in 1889 wanted to try the food of the people, and chose this simple version as her favourite. Allegedly, she was patriotically attracted by the tomatoes, mozzarella cheese, oregano and basil of its topping, reflecting the red, white and green of the Italian flag.

Italian staple

When southern Italian families moved to the industrialised north in search of work in the 1950s and 1960s, they took their favourite food with them. Today, an estimated 7 million pizzas are made and sold in Italy every day.

Other authentic Neapolitan pizzas include *napoletana*, made with tomatoes, mozzarella, and anchovies; *marinara*, a simple combination of fresh tomatoes and juicy new-season's garlic, and *quattro stagioni*, the famous Four Seasons, divided into quarters with anchovy strips, then piled high with a variety of toppings.

REGIONAL SPECIALITIES

At a typical restaurant the waiter will point out the day's specials. Usually they will be the best bargain. Look around and see what others are eating.

Starters might include *crostini*, toasted rounds of bread topped with tomato, mozzarella and anchovy, sometimes with chicken livers. Baked peppers are stuffed with chopped olives, capers and anchovies *(peperoni ripieni)*, or roasted and peeled, then simply bathed in light olive oil and topped with anchovies. *Mozzarella in carrozza* is sliced cheese sandwiched in bread, then dipped in beaten egg and lightly fried. For a lighter start to the meal choose *insalata caprese*, a tomato, mozzarella and fresh basil salad from Capri. Deep-fried squid *(calamaretti)* and whitebait *(cecenielli)* make tasty starters, and there is always

Sweet pasteria napoletana is eaten at Easter

salami and the northern standby, thinly sliced Parma ham (*prosciutto*) with melon or fresh figs (*fichi*).

Seafood is popular throughout the region. Naples is renowned for its *fritto misto di mare*, a huge pile of mixed fish deep-fried in a light and crispy batter. Lobster (*aragosta*) or big grilled prawns (*gamberi*) can be your reward after a hard day's sunbathing. *Zuppa di pesce*, a delicious assortment of seafood cooked with tomatoes, garlic and spices, makes a meal in itself. *Triglie*, little red mullet, are good fried, while *spigola* (sea bass) is excellent grilled. The best restaurants will present the fish for your approval before cooking it and will charge according to the weight. Fresh fish can be expensive: confirm the price to avoid surprises when the bill comes.

Main courses are often simple, flavoursome stews and roasts, such as *coniglio all'ischitana*, an Ischian speciality of rabbit stewed in the local white wine with tomatoes and rosemary, or *spezzatino*, a veal stew with vegetables. More elaborate, Sicilian-influenced dishes may be available – a remnant of Naples' royal past. Beef steaks are not the best choice in the South, but pork (*maiale*) is a better bet, such as chops (*costolette*) with rosemary.

For **dessert**, fresh fruit might include strawberries (*fragole*), a fruit salad (*macedonia di frutta*), or fresh pears (*pere*) with creamy gorgonzola and mascarpone cheeses. In a truly *di lusso* (deluxe) establishment such as Capri's Hotel Quisisana, orange segments (*arance*) in orange liqueur may be prepared at your table with Neapolitan flair: the waiter peels it in one unbroken spiral, then cuts out the segments, squeezes the juice from the membrane with a fork and arranges the segments like flower petals. If you want something more indulgent, there are more elaborate desserts such as *coviglie al caffè*, a rich, coffee-flavoured cream.

Naples' famous pastries are to be found in *pasticcerie* or bar/caffès, rather than on a restaurant's dessert menu. The mouth-watering selection of **cakes** include classic Campanian Easter cake (*pastiera*) made from fresh wheat grains, ricotta, and candied fruits; *sfogliatelle*, light, crisp pastries with various fillings, popular at breakfast time; and the incredibly sticky *struffoli*, like doughnuts drenched in honey.

Naples is famous for its delicious **ices** and **ice creams**; it is fun to sample these at a *gelateria*, where glorious pastries are also displayed. A *granita di caffè* or *limone* is a strongly flavoured ice shaved from frozen coffee or lemonade. Try the coffee *con panna* – with whipped cream.

COFFEE

The beans for Italian coffee may come from the same sources as French, British, American or Turkish coffee, but what a difference! It's all in the roasting. Italian *espresso* is seemingly impossible to duplicate anywhere else, even with imported Italian *espresso* machines. With hot steam-foamed milk added to the cup and dusted with powdered chocolate, it's a *cappuccino*, brown and hooded like a Capuchin friar. With just a drop of hot milk it becomes a *caffè macchiato* (a 'stained' *espresso*).

WINES

The wines of Campania are rarely exported, though they are becoming more popular. Perhaps the best are the whites of Ischia, which are good with seafood and antipasti, and Greco di Tufo, another dry white produced on the mainland, as well as the full-bodied Taurasi and Falerno reds. Capri produces small quantities of its own light, dry white wine, and even smaller amounts of red. Irpinia is an excellent local wine, available in red or white, and Ravello's red and rosé are renowned regionally. For every day, just say *rosso* to go with your pasta and you'll probably get a Gragnano. From the slopes of Vesuvius itself comes the mournfully named Lacryma Christi (Tears of Christ). The local house wine is usually a safe bet: see what the locals are ordering.

Finish the meal with a digestif of icy cold *limoncello*, made from Amalfitana lemons and drunk straight from the freezer. *Buon appetito*!

TO HELP YOU ORDER

I'd like a table. **Vorrei un tavolo.**
Do you have a set menu? **Avete un menù a prezzo fisso?**
I'd like... **Vorrei...**

beer **una birra**
bread **del pane**
butter **del burro**
coffee **un caffè**
cream **della panna**

fork **una forchetta**
glass **un bicchiere**
ice cream **un gelato**
knife **un coltello**
pepper **del pepe**

potatoes **delle patate**
salad **dell'insalata**
salt **del sale**
soup **una minestra**
spoon **un cucchiaio**
sugar **dello zucchero**
tea **un tè**
wine **del vino**

MENU READER

acciughe anchovies
aglio garlic
agnello lamb
albicocche apricots
arancia orange
arrosto roast
braciola chop
calamari squid
calzone folded pizza
carciofi artichokes
cipolle onions
coniglio rabbit
cozze mussels
crostacei shellfish
fagiolini green beans
fiche figs
finocchio fennel
formaggio cheese
frittata omelette
frutti di mare seafood
funghi mushrooms
gamberi prawns

Limoncello liqueur

limone lemon
melanzane aubergine
maiale pork
peperoni peppers
pesca peach
pesce fish
pollo chicken
polpo octopus
pomodoro tomato
salsa sauce
sogliola sole
spinaci spinach
tonno tuna
torta cake
uova eggs
vongole clams

PLACES TO EAT

We have used the following symbols to give an idea of the price for a three-course meal for one, including wine, cover and service:

€€€   over 50 euros
€€   25–50 euros
€   below 25 euros

NAPLES

Amici Miei €€ *Via Monte di Dio 78, Chiaia, tel: 081-764 6063*, www.ristorante amicimiei.com. Small, dark and intimate restaurant, long loved for its meat specialities and classic pastas. This being Naples, fresh seafood is given its fair share of attentive preparation: no one leaves disappointed, especially after sampling the homemade fruit tarts. Lunch and dinner Tuesday–Saturday, Sunday lunch only; closed July & Aug.

Brandi € *Salita S. Anna di Palazzo (corner of Via Chiaia), tel: 081-416928*, www.brandi.it. Never mind that the pizza Margherita (the classic version with mozzarella and tomato sauce named after King Umberto's queen) is said to have been born here in 1889. This is Naples' oldest pizzeria (with a full trattoria menu), and still one of its most frequented, by celebs (signed photos plastered everywhere), locals and tourists alike. Cosy and bustling indoors, with a few tables outside on a narrow alleyway. Open for lunch and dinner daily.

Chalet Ciro € *Via Francesco Caracciolo 31, Mergellina, tel: 081-669 928*, www.chaletciro.it. Italy is famed for its ice cream and Neapolitans will cross the city to queue at this seafront *gelateria/pasticceria* near the Mergellina ferry. It's home to probably the most famous ice cream in Naples, with a huge array of flavours and a sea view while you slurp. Open 7am–2.30am, closed Wed.

Ciro a Santa Brigida €€ *Via Santa Brigida 71, tel: 081-552 4072*, www.ciro asantabrigida.it. Since opening in 1932, this has been an institution for regulars including Toscanini and Pirandello. Off the store-lined Via Toledo, the two-storey restaurant is always busy. Offers pizzas or a lengthy menu of classic Neapolitan dishes served by *simpatico* house-proud waiters. Open for lunch and dinner Mon–Sat.

Caffè Gambrinus € *Via Chiaia 1–2, tel: 081-417582,* www.grancaffegambrinus.com. The city's most famous and theatrical *caffè*, this 19th-century landmark near the Palazzo Reale is still a stylish watering hole for all strata of local society and intelligentsia, as well as savvy visitors who enjoy the people-watching. Light meals, famous pastries and ice creams, or just a coffee or cappuccino secure a table at the grandly vaulted indoor salons or outdoors. A pianist or Viennese orchestra add to the experience. Open Sun–Thu 7am–1am, Fri 7am–2am, Sat 7am–3am.

Di Matteo € *Via dei Tribunali 94, tel: 081-455 262,* www.pizzeriadimatteo.com. Brandi may have the history and glamour, but in the fiercely contested battle for the finest pizza in Naples (and thus the world), local aficionados are placing this simple pizzeria just ahead of nearby Da Michele (also fabulous). Prepare to queue. No credit cards accepted. Open Mon–Sat 8.30am–midnight.

La Locanda del Grifo € *Via F. Del Giudice 14; tel: 081-557 1492,* www.lalocandadelgrifo.com. This pizzeria-restaurant enjoys a fantastic central location, with outdoor tables on a cobbled Centro Storico square just off hectic Via dei Tribunali. The huge pizzas are the draw here, but the menu also offers a handful of *secondi*. Look out for the griffin that gives the restaurant its name, perched on the campanile opposite. Open for lunch and dinner daily.

Palazzo Petrucci €€€ *Piazza San Domenico Maggiore 5–7, tel: 081-551 2460,* www.palazzopetrucci.it. A gourmet heaven in the former stable block of a 17th-century palazzo at the heart of the Centro Storico, offering a Michelin-starred variation on Neapolitan cuisine in simple but elegant surroundings. Closed most of Aug, Sun dinner, Mon lunch, and Sun–Mon lunch Jun–Jul.

Scaturchio € *Piazza San Domenico Maggiore 19, tel: 081-551 7031,* www.scaturchio.it. A wonderfully atmospheric affair that is the quintessential Neapolitan bar/*pasticceria*, this venerable century-old landmark showcases the local art of pastry making at its best. Policemen, nuns, hipsters and grandmothers come here for excellent coffee and local specialities such as *babà al rhum*, *sfogliatelle* stuffed with sweetened ricotta cheese, and *ministeriale*, a chocolate cake with whipped rum-cream filling. Open daily 7.20am–8.20pm. No credit cards.

La Scialuppa €€ *Borgo Marinaro 4, tel: 081-764 5333.* One of the most charming of the many traditional seafood restaurants in the fishermen's quarter at the foot of Castel dell'Ovo. Sit beside the water listening to the buskers, watching the yachts and eating luscious fresh pasta with seafood and scarlet cherry tomatoes. Lunch and dinner, closed Mon.

CAPRI

Aurora €€€ *Via Fuorlovado 18–20, Capri Town, tel: 081-837 0181*, www. auroracapri.com. The Neapolitan tradition of pizza as an art form lives on here. A simple pizza and a home-made dessert make for a memorable meal, as confirmed by all the celebs whose autographed glossies grace the walls of this old-time favourite. Also offers full restaurant menu and extensive wine list. Open for lunch and dinner daily Mar–Dec.

La Capannina €€ *Via Le Botteghe 12bis, Capri Town, tel: 081-837 0732*, www.capanninacapri.it. Located a brief stroll from the town's principal Piazzetta, this well-loved spot for local specialities attracts celebrity guests who enjoy good, unpretentious dining in the pergola-covered courtyard. The house wine from the owner's island vineyard pairs deliciously with homemade pasta and fresh fish. Open daily for lunch and dinner, mid-Mar–mid-Jan. Closed Wed off-season.

La Fontelina €€ *I Faraglioni (at the end of Via Tragara), Capri Town, tel: 081-837 0845*, www.fontelina-capri.com. Overlooking the dramatic off-shore Faraglioni, this idyllic little beach club and restaurant serves lunch only on breezy bamboo-shaded terraces, with its own patch of rocky beach below. Fresh and refreshing, the fruit-filled white wine sangria sets the tone for a simple and delicious menu of homemade pasta and the best of the local fish market's morning delivery. Its competitor, Da Luigi, is just next door, with an equally impressive setting and slightly more expensive menu. Open daily for lunch only, mid-Apr–mid-Oct.

Da Gelsomina €€ *Via Migliara 72, Anacapri, tel: 081-837 1499,* www.da gelsomina.com. Part of a six-room *pensione* hideaway, this charming countryside spot with sweeping views is best for a leisurely lunch. Its *ravioli alla caprese* and homemade wine from its surrounding vineyard are two of many reasons to come here. Open daily for lunch and dinner mid-June–mid-Sept; closed mid-Nov–Mar; dinner only mid-Apr–mid-Oct.

Da Paolino €€€ *Via Palazzo a Mare 11, Marina Grande, tel: 081-837 6102,* www.paolinocapri.com. You may find yourself fighting Hollywood A-listers for a table at one of Italy's most romantic restaurants, where the candlelit tables, piled high with mouth-watering *antipasti*, are set amidst the lemon groves. Save up for a splurge. Open daily Apr–Oct, dinner only Apr–May. Book ahead.

Terrazza Brunella €€€ *Via Tragara 24; tel: 081-837 0122,* www.terrazza brunella.com. Near Punta Tragara, a 10–15 minute walk from the Piazzetta, is this atmospheric restaurant, with a spectacular clifftop setting offering incredible views – book in advance to get one of the tables by the window. The food is excellent, if pricey: try the lobster linguine or the king prawns with cognac. Open daily for lunch and dinner Easter–Oct.

SORRENTO

L'Antica Trattoria €€€ *Via Padre R Giuliani 33 (Piazza Tasso), tel: 081-807 1082,* www.lanticatrattoria.com. An oasis of charm in what is a surprising foodie desert. This pretty little restaurant has been offering gourmet versions of local favourites in a flower-filled courtyard just off Piazza Tasso since 1930, to the accompaniment of a mandolin in the evenings. Open for lunch and dinner daily; closed Mon in winter. Book ahead.

Bagni Delfino €€ *via Marina Grande 216, tel: 081-878 2038.* A large family-run establishment down in the harbour with an outdoor terrace, Delfino's has been serving up both seafood and foreigner-friendly smiles in copious quantities since 1938. It also has its own bathing platform filled with rows of sunbeds that ensure it is a popular hangout for tourists. Open for lunch and dinner daily.

Don Alfonso 1890 €€€ *Corso Sant'Agata 11–13, Sant'Agata sui Due Golfi, tel: 081-878 0026,* www.donalfonso.com. Pilgrims of gastronomy know the 7km (4.3-mile) drive from Sorrento to the hills 365m (1,200ft) above sea level is a price willingly paid for a meal at one of Italy's finest and most renowned restaurants. The proud holder of two Michelin stars, the restaurant serves an inventive, regionally influenced cuisine, using exquisite ingredients that come largely from the owners' farm. The award-winning wine cellar is one of the largest and best in Italy. Serious food and wine lovers will love this elegant and expensive experience, as well as the warmth of the gracious Iaccarino family, who have run a restaurant here for over 100 years. There are rooms if you wish to stay. Open mid-Apr–Oct, lunch and dinner. Closed Mon and Tue (open Tue evening mid-June–mid-Sept). Advance booking essential.

POSITANO

Da Adolfo € *Via Laurito 40, tel: 089-875022,* www.daadolfo.com. A seductive glimpse of *la dolce vita* endures effortlessly at this casual outdoor restaurant reached only by motorboat (from Positano's main pier every 30 minutes 10am–1pm). Come for a simple, superbly fresh meal of home-cooked pasta, grilled mozzarella wrapped in lemon leaves and grilled fish, then hire a lounge chair or umbrella for a few idyllic hours on the beach. Open for lunch daily, May–mid-Oct. No credit cards.

Buca di Bacco €€ *Via Rampa Teglia 8, tel: 089-875699,* www.bucadibacco. it. Together with Chez Black, one of the most enduring of the beachfront see-and-be-seen scenes, this second-storey arbour-covered restaurant has made great strides to recoup some of its fading reputation. Its best main courses are the simply grilled fresh fish. Book early for the railing-side tables with a view of the action below. A pre-dinner drink at the first-floor open-sided bar is de rigueur. Open daily for lunch and dinner. Closed Nov–mid-Mar.

Chez Black €€€ *Via del Brigantino 19, tel: 089-875036,* www.chezblack.it. A stylish 'in' restaurant that is one of a cluster snuggled directly on the beach. It offers very good quality food and value-for-money considering its prime location and long-time popularity. For an informal lunch or relaxed dinner, it is one of the better choices in town for great pizzas and pastas, with reliably fresh fish for more serious dining. Open daily Mar–early Jan.

Ristorante da Costantino €€ *Via Montepertuso 107, tel: 089-875 738,* www.dacostantino.net. Dizzyingly high up the cliff at the back of the town, this unpretentious neighbourhood restaurant envelopes you like a warm hug from an old friend, feeds you on good traditional food and, unless you suffer from vertigo, offers a 6-star view. One of very few to stay open all year.

AMALFI

La Caravella €€€ *Via Matteo Camera 12, tel: 089-871029,* www.ristorante lacaravella.it. A throwback to when the *dolce vita* jet-set put Amalfi on the holiday circuit. The Art Deco decor is the setting for what is still considered one of the area's most serious restaurants. A tasting menu familiarises guests with the coastline's specialities as interpreted by a nouvelle cuisine-inspired kitchen. Open for lunch and dinner daily; closed Tue and mid-Jan–mid-Feb.

Pasticceria Savoia € *2 Via Camero Matteo, tel: 089-871 445,* www.savoia pasticceria.it. This boutique *pasticceria* in the heart of Amalfi is an essential stop for foodies. Owned by the Amatruda family, it is famous for its *sfogliatella* and traditional *cannoli* filled with cream and chocolate. They also serve a great variety of *gelati*, including more unusual combinations like ricotta with pear. Open daily 7.30am–11.30pm. Closed end-Jan–Feb.

Da Gemma €€€ *Via Fra Gerardo Sasso 11, tel: 089-871345,* www.trattoria dagemma.com. One of the town's favourites for more than 100 years, this family-owned restaurant sits a short walk from the cathedral, and has a second-storey open terrace that overlooks the main street. Pastas are prepared with tomato-based sauces and added to seafood, and a thick *zuppa di pesce* (fish soup) is one of the recommended main-course specialities. Open daily for lunch and dinner. Closed mid-Jan–mid-Feb and Wed.

RAVELLO

Cumpà Cosimo €€ *Via Roma 44, tel: 089-857156*. The best (and best known) eatery in town for good home cooking and trattoria ambience. Regional dishes are served in generous proportions with many ingredients sourced from the family farm. A series of seven different sample-size pastas, each more delicious than the last, leaves little room for the mixed grill of fish, or any of the meat specialities from the owner's butcher's shop next door. Open daily for lunch and dinner; closed Mon off-season. Closed mid-Jan–mid-Mar.

Villa Maria €€ *Via Santa Chiara 2, tel: 089-857255,* www.villamaria.it. Relaxed yet refined, this is one of the prettiest settings for lunch with a bird's-eye panorama, or for dinner with a high romance quotient. Classical music drifts through the pergola-covered alfresco terrace and cosy indoor dining room of this century-old villa that also offers a dozen rooms. The chef knows his regional specialities, beginning with the homemade spaghetti-like *scialatielli*. Open daily for lunch and dinner; winter closures vary.

A–Z TRAVEL TIPS

A SUMMARY OF PRACTICAL INFORMATION

A

ACCOMMODATION (see also Camping; Youth Hostels)

The government-controlled star-rating system for accommodation descends from five to one. In Naples and the main resorts, amenities are spartan below three stars, but further afield more modest hotels and *pensioni* can be cosy bargains and there are some good *agriturismi* in the surrounding countryside. Hotel recommendations are listed on page 134. Make sure to book ahead if you are visiting in peak season.

AIRPORT

Naples' airport is at Capodichino, 7km (4 miles) from the city centre; tel: 848 888 777 or +39 081-789 6111 from abroad; www.aeroporto-dinapoli.it.

For lost baggage assistance, tel: 081 1949 4055.

There is limited duty-free shopping for travellers from outside the EU. Tourist information offices and banking facilities are in the arrival area. Allow at least 20 minutes for the taxi ride from the airport to the centre of Naples (see Budgeting for Your Trip for fares). The Alibus bus (www.anm.it) service runs regularly (every 20–30mins) to Piazza Garibaldi (15–20 mins) and on to Piazza Municipio (30–35 mins). Purchase tickets on the bus (€4) or inside the terminal (where the cost is €3). Curreri buses (www.curreriviaggi.it) run every 75 minutes to Sorrento from outside arrivals (1hr 15 mins); the same bus stops at Pompeii on request.

B

BICYCLE HIRE

Hiring a bicycle or scooter is possible in some resort towns and the islands. Some mechanics may rent you a scooter in Naples, but it is best to avoid this experience.

BUDGETING FOR YOUR TRIP

Here are some average prices in euros, based on high-season rates:

Airport transfer. Taxis from the airport into town charge around €19, to Piazza Garibaldi €16, to Vomero or Chiaia €23.

Camping. €5–12 per person per day.

Entertainment. Cinema: €5–9. Concert: €10–100.

Guides. (for 1–20 persons). Full day, €100; half day, €50.

Guided tours. Half-day trip to Pompeii, €50; full-day, Pompeii, Sorrento and Amalfi drive, €90, with lunch; boat to Blue Grotto, €15–25.

Meals and drinks. Continental breakfast, €7–20; lunch/dinner, €20–60; coffee €0.80–1.20 at the bar, €2–3 served at table; carafe of house wine from €4; beer €2; soft drink €1.50; aperitif €3–9.

Museums. €4–17. The Artecard offers free or discounted entry to museums in Naples or throughout the region. Prices range from €21 for three days in the city centre to €34 for seven days across the region. They can be purchased from museums, tourist offices and newsagents, by calling 800-600 601 (tel: 06-399-67650 from abroad), or online at www.campaniartecard.it.

Transport. City bus, metro and funicular, €1.50 for 90 min, €4.50 per day (€5.80 for weekly pass); taxi, meter starts at €3.50, surcharges after 10pm and on Sundays and holidays; train to Pompeii, €6.40 return; boat to Capri or Ischia, €18 single; petrol, around €1.53 per litre. Arte Card Campagnia allows 72hrs of travel on the rail system throughout Campania for €32, as well as city transport.

Youth Hostel. €15 per person per night (without breakfast).

C

CAMPING

There are campsites near Naples, by the Solfatara at Pozzuoli, all over the Phlegrean Fields, on the flanks of Vesuvius at Torre del Greco and Trecase, near Sorrento, on Ischia and on the shore near Paestum. Full details of sites are provided in the guide *Campeggi e Villaggi Turistici* (www.campeggievillaggi.it), published annually by the Italian Touring Club (TCI). Federcampeggio's free list of sites, with location map, is available from tourist offices (see page 131) or from Federcampeggio (tel: 055-882391; www.federcampeggio.it). A list of campsites in Naples and surrounding areas can be found at www.camping.it/en/campania/napoli. Most campsites are closed Nov–Apr; one exception is the Naples Complesso Turistico Averno site near the beach in Pozzuoli (tel: 081-8042666; www.averno.it).

CAR HIRE (see also Driving)

All the major car-hire companies have outlets at the airport. Be sure to take a major credit card as cash is not always accepted. Car hire is not cheap in Italy due to the high accident rate, with prices starting at around €55 a day in high season. Always check that the quoted rate includes Collision Damage Waiver, unlimited mileage and tax. Cheap deals may come with a huge excess. Consider taking out a cheaper annual policy to ensure your excess with Insurance4CarHire (www.insurance4carhire.com); it can save a fortune. To hire a car you must be over 21 and have held a full driving licence for at least 12 months.

Avis has offices at the airport, central station and Via Piedigrotta; tel: 081-761 8354, www.avis.co.uk; Europcar is at the airport tel: 081-780 5643 and Corso Meridionale 60/62 tel: 081-764 9838, www.europcar.com; Hertz is at the airport tel: 081-231 1200, central station tel: 081-202 860, www.hertz.com; Sixt is at the airport tel: 081-751 2055 and the railway station tel: 039 06652111, www.sixt.com; Maggiore is at the airport tel: 081-780 3011, and central station, tel: 081-287858, www.maggiore.it.

CLIMATE

The weather in Naples and its nearby resorts is mild year-round. In July–August, the average high is 33°C (92°F), though heat waves are not uncommon; the average minimum in January–February is 2°C

(35ºF). Spring and autumn are the best seasons to visit, mainly because they are less crowded. Mid-August, *ferragosto*, is when most Italian families take their holidays and the coastal areas are packed. Daily average temperatures:

	J	F	M	A	M	J	J	A	S	O	N	D
ºC	8	9	11	14	17	21	24	24	21	17	13	10
ºF	46	48	52	57	63	70	75	75	70	63	56	50

CLOTHING

Few restaurants in Naples require a jacket and tie, though they are required in one or two elegant places in the evening. As for the islands and coasts, pretty much anything goes, and Capri at night is designer heaven. Shorts and skimpy T-shirts and dresses are frowned on in churches, and are not allowed in large cathedrals. Lightweight clothing and a fold-up umbrella are sufficient during most of the year, but from November to March the Bay of Naples can be damp and chilly between days of sunshine. Bring a raincoat and warm sweater in winter. You will need comfortable hiking shoes for climbing Vesuvius and exploring ruins. A hat and sunglasses are necessary in the summer.

CRIME AND SAFETY

Despite its reputation as a hotbed of crime, Naples is no more dangerous than any other large European city if you take the usual precautions. The main problems tourists experience are pickpocketing and bag-snatching, together with theft from parked cars. To prevent petty thieves from spoiling your holiday, carry no more cash than the minimum needed for transport, meals and tickets. Use credit cards for larger purchases. Don't carry a handbag or camera bag loosely slung over your street-side shoulder (thieves on motorbikes or in cars have been known to cut these off in drive-bys). Make photocopies of all documents and travellers' cheques to leave in your luggage in the eventuality of a theft.

Never leave anything of value in your car when parked, not even in the boot; wherever possible, park in a garage or attended parking area. Never put items in the back window of a car, whether parked or in traffic. Leave valuables you don't need every day in the hotel safe; don't carry your hotel key with you outside the hotel. Don't wear conspicuous expensive jewellery; never let your bags out of sight in stations and public places. If you travel by train, keep the door and windows of sleeping-car compartments locked at night.

> I want to report a theft. **Voglio denunciare un furto**.
> My wallet/handbag/passport/ticket has been stolen.
> **Mi hanno rubato il portafoglio/la borsa/il passaporto/ il biglietto**.

D

DRIVING

Motorists taking their vehicle into Italy need a full driving licence with a translation, an International Motor Insurance Certificate and a Vehicle Registration Document. A green insurance card is not a legal requirement, but is strongly recommended.

The use of seat belts in front and back seats is obligatory; fines for non-compliance are stiff. A red warning triangle must be carried in case of breakdown. Motorcycle riders must wear crash helmets. The ACI (Automobile Club d'Italia; www.aci.it) gives some online information worth consulting before you set off.

Driving conditions. Drive on the right, and give way to traffic coming from the right. Speed limits: 50kph (30mph) in town, 90kph (55mph) on freeways (*superstrade*) and 130kph (80mph) on motorways (*autostrade*), the latter being toll roads. The roads of the Sorrento peninsula are serpentine and filled with hire cars whose drivers are as unfamiliar with the road as you. The Amalfi Coast is so congested it becomes one-way in high summer and you have to drive right round the peninsula if you take a wrong turn.

Rules and regulations. Italian traffic police (*polizia stradale*) can impose on-the-spot fines for speeding and traffic offences. All cities and many towns have signs posted at the outskirts indicating the phone number of the local traffic police headquarters or *carabinieri* (see Police).

Road signs. Most road signs in Italy are international. Here are some written signs you might come across:

Curva pericolosa Dangerous bend/curve
Deviazione Detour
Divieto di sorpasso No passing
Divieto di sosta No stopping
Pericolo Danger
Rallentare Slow down
Senso vietato/unico No entry/One-way street
Vietato l'ingresso No entry
Zona pedonale Pedestrian zone
Please fill the tank with super/unleaded/diesel **Per favore, faccia il pieno di super/senza piombo/gasolio**
I've had a breakdown. **Ho avuto un guasto.**
There's been an accident. **C'è stato un incidente.**

Fuel. Petrol (*benzina*) is sold as Super and Unleaded (*senza piombo* or SP). Diesel is called *gasolio*. It is illegal to carry spare fuel in your car. Petrol stations are generally open 7am–12.30pm and 3–7.30pm. Many have self-service (look for a '24' sign) via an automatic payment machine, which accepts euro notes, and often credit/debit cards. Service stations on the *autostrada* are manned 24 hours a day.

Parking. In Naples, parking (posteggio/parcheggio) is so difficult and there are so few car parks that it is hardly worth driving. Self-explanatory signs indicate tow-away zones (*zona di rimozione*) where parked cars will be whisked away in minutes. If this happens to you, find the nearest traffic policeman. Street parking costs €2–5, though in Naples supervised parking is a must. Car parks (*parcheggio*) are marked with a blue 'P'. The most convenient is at the port, Molo Beverello (tel: 335-499 658; www.parcheggiobeverello.com; open 24 hours a day). You can also park along blue lines in the city-centre from Mon–Sat but the rates are steep. One-hour parking on Sun and holidays is slightly cheaper.

E

ELECTRICITY

220v/50Hz AC is standard. The sockets are 2-round pin continental style but the pins are slimmer than some adapters on sale at airports; American 110v appliances also require a transformer.

EMBASSIES AND CONSULATES

Australia: 5 Via Antonio Bosio, Rome; tel: 06-852 721; www.italy.embassy. gov.au

Canada: 30 Via Zara, Rome; tel: 06-854 441; www.canadainternational. gc.ca/italy-italie

Ireland: Villa Spada, Via Giacomo Medici, Rome; tel: 06-585 2381; www. dfa.ie/irish-embassy/italy/

New Zealand: 44 Via Clitunno, Rome; tel: 06-853 7501; www.mfat.govt. nz

UK: 80a Via XX Settembre, Rome; tel: 06-4220 0001; www.gov.uk

US: Piazza della Repubblica, Naples; tel: 081-5838 111; https://it.us embassy.gov/

EMERGENCIES

The National Emergency Number: 112

Police **113**

Fire brigade **115**

Ambulance **118**

If you don't speak Italian, find a local resident to help you, or talk to an English-speaking operator by dialling **170**.

> Can you please place an emergency call... **Per favore, può fare una telefonata d'emergenza...**
> to the police? **alla polizia?**
> to the fire brigade? **ai vigili del fuoco?**
> to the hospital? **all'ospedale?**

G

GAY AND LESBIAN TRAVELLERS

Naples is as gay-friendly as any of Italy's large cities – which is to say relatively. The coastline resorts, particularly Positano and Capri, have long attracted gay northern-Italian holidaymakers from the fashion and art worlds. Arcigay, the national gay rights organisation is a great source for finding bars, beaches and other gay-friendly localities. Contact Arcigay Napoli, Vico San Geronimo alle Monache 19, tel: 081-552 8815, www.arcigaynapoli.org. Also visit www.gay.it for updated information. The magazine *Spartacus International Gay Guide* can be found at newsstands.

GETTING THERE

By air. Capodichino Airport is served by direct flights from many European cities, including London Stansted and Gatwick with British Airways (www.ba.com) and easyJet (www.easyjet.com). In summer, charter flights add to the schedule.

By rail. Naples is on the fast European sleeper and express train lines, with through trains to major Italian cities, European capitals and connections with Rome at least once an hour (1hr 10 min–3 hour journey).

Children under the age of four travel free (unless individual accommodation is required); children aged four to 12 pay half fare. Tickets can be purchased and reservations made at travel agencies and railway stations. For train information dial 89 20 21 (a local call throughout Italy; English-speaking operators) or visit www.trenitalia.com, which has an international internet booking system.

The best Italian trains (*treni*) are the *frecce*; these super-fast trains are replacing the older Eurostar services. Frecciarossa trains connect Turin, Milan, Bologna, Rome, Naples and Salerno. Intercity trains are less fast and connect major and minor cities. The local Regionale services make many stops and tend to be very slow. For the faster trains, fares are cheaper the earlier you buy your ticket, and cheaper still if you don't require flexibility.

In Naples, trains to international and national destinations (other than the Cumana and Circumflegrea suburban lines) leave from the Stazione Centrale in Piazza Garibaldi.

By car. Rome is 220km (137 miles) away by *autostrada* (motorway).

By coach. In addition to the comprehensive, inexpensive, but rather slow intercity bus services linking Naples to the rest of Italy, express coaches from Rome serve Naples and, in the summer, Sorrento and Positano. Consult Tourist Information Points on Via San Carlo 9, Piazza del Gesù or Piazza del Plebiscito. Regional coach tours are operated by tour companies in most European countries. National Express Eurolines runs coaches from London Victoria to Naples (tel: 08717 818 178 in the UK; to book in Naples, tel: 0861-199 1900; www.eurolines.com).

By sea. If your destination is an island or seaside resort, hydrofoil services and passenger ferries leave Naples regularly from the Molo Beverello docks by the Castel Nuovo. The trip to Capri, Ischia or Sorrento takes 30–60 mins. There are usually hydrofoils to the Amalfi Coast in summer; see www.metrodelmare.it. Larger car ferries also leave for Sardinia, Sicily's Aeolian Islands and Palermo.

GUIDES AND TOURS

Guided tours of Naples and the surrounding area can be arranged through Giro Città, tel: 081-248 8315. Guides who offer services at tourist sites, such as Pompeii or the National Archaeological Museum, should be asked to show their credentials. Every Thursday, Saturday and Sunday the official Naples tourist organisation conducts three tours of a different church or site. For information, tel: 081-400256, www.lanapoli sotterranea.it. City Sightseeing Napoli (tel: 081-551 7279, www.napoli. city-sightseeing.it) operates a hop-on, hop-off bus with commentary in eight languages; tickets last 24hrs. Tour Guides Naples (mobile: +39 33 88 884 282; www.tourguidenaples.com) is a group of accredited tour guides that offers private tours of the city and bay area. **Context Travel** offers small-group and private walking and car tours led by art historians and archaeologists (tel: 06-4890 0042 or toll free 1 800 691 6036, www.contexttravel.com).

H

HEALTH AND MEDICAL CARE

EU residents should obtain the European Health Insurance Card, available in the UK from post offices or online (www.ehic.org.uk), which entitles them to emergency medical treatment on the same terms as Italians. To cover all eventualities, medical insurance is recommended. Non-EU visitors must pay for medical care and medicine, and should have medical insurance. There are few health risks other than sunburn. Ask your consulate or hotel to recommend an English-speaking doctor or dentist, or a clinic.

Where's the nearest (all-night) pharmacy? **Dov'è la farmacia (di turno) più vicina?**
I need a doctor/dentist. **Ho bisogno di un medico/dentista.**

Chemists (*farmacie*) follow shop hours and close for lunch, but they take turns as the *farmacia di turno*, open night and day. The addresses of pharmacies on duty appear on every chemist's door and in local papers. In Italy, pharmacists can often provide medication that at home would require a prescription. The pharmacy at Napoli Centrale station is open 7am–10pm. You can find on-duty pharmacies at www.farmaciediturno.net.

HOLIDAYS

Banks, government offices, most shops and some museums and galleries are closed on the following days. When one falls on a Thursday or a Tuesday, Italians may make a *ponte* (bridge) to the weekend, meaning that Friday or Monday is taken off as well.

1 January *Capodanno* New Year's Day
6 January *Epifania* Epiphany
25 April *Festa della Liberazione* Liberation Day
1 May *Festa del Lavoro* Labour Day
14 May *San Costanzo* St Constance (Capri)
13 June *Sant'Antonio* St Anthony (Anacapri)
15 August *Ferragosto* Assumption Day
19 September *San Gennaro* Patron Saint of Naples
1 November *Ognissanti* All Saint's Day
8 December *L'Immacolata Concezione* Immaculate Conception
25 December *Natale* Christmas Day
26 December *Santo Stefano* St Stephen's Day
Movable dates
Pasqua Easter Sunday
Lunedi di Pasqua Easter Monday

L

LANGUAGE

Your efforts to speak a few words of Italian will win smiles and cooperation. Also, many Italians are studying English and are keen to try it out on visitors. The Neopolitan dialect is impenetrable, even to northern Italians. Bear in mind the following tips on Italian pronunciation:

c is pronounced like ch in 'charge' when followed by an e or an i, as in cello = ˈchelloˈ and *arriverderci* = ˈariverder-cheeˈ

ch sounds like k

g followed by an e or an i has a j sound, as in ˈjetˈ

gh sounds like g in ˈgoˈ

gl followed by i sounds like lli in ˈmillionˈ

gn is pronounced like ny in ˈcanyonˈ, eg agnello = ˈan-yellowˈ

sc before e and i is pronounced sh as in ˈshipˈ

The *Berlitz Italian Phrase Book and Dictionary* covers all the situations you are likely to encounter; it includes a pronunciation guide, basic grammar and 3,500-word dictionary.

Do you speak English? **Parla inglese?**
I don't speak Italian. **Non parlo italiano.**

MAPS

There are so many tiny alleys in Naples, they can't all fit on a map, or at least on the free ones available from the Information Office on Piazza del Gesù. Maps of the area can be found at newsstands and bookshops, including the excellent Touring Club of Italy maps.

I'd like a street map of... **Vorrei una piantina di...**

MEDIA

Newspapers and Magazines. In Naples, the kiosks run out of foreign publications early. If you are staying for some time and want your favourite paper regularly, order it or ask your hotel to do so. In Capri the kiosk in the central Piazzetta has a good selection, and the same is true in other resort towns. The free monthly *Qui Napoli*, a compilation of all visitor-necessary information, is distributed in most hotels and is available to download from www.inaples.it. The best local newspaper for listings is *Il Mattino*.

Radio and TV. The Italian state TV network, RAI, has three TV channels, which compete with six independent channels. All programmes are in Italian, including British and American programmes, which are dubbed. CNN (in English) is transmitted on TMC from 4.20–6am and from 3.15am on Sundays. Most hotels and hired properties have cable connections. The nearby NATO base broadcasts English programmes all day on 106 and 107FM.

MONEY

Currency. Italy's currency is the euro. Notes are denominated in 5, 10, 20, 50, 100 and 500 euros; coins in 1 and 2 euros and 1, 2, 5, 10, 20 and 50 cents.

Banks and currency exchange. Banks give the best exchange rates, although exchange offices are almost as good and have the benefit of longer opening hours. Don't forget to take your passport when changing travellers' cheques.

ATMs. Check with your bank before departure how much they charge for withdrawing money from ATMs (cash dispensers) on your credit or debit card.

Credit cards. These are accepted in most hotels and larger shops in the Naples area, as indicated on their door. However, don't expect cards to be taken by market traders, small village shops and some trattorias.

Where is the bank? **Dov'è la banca?**
Where is an ATM? **Dov'è il bancomat?**

Travellers' cheques. These are rarely used these days. You should exchange your cheques for euros at a bank or *cambio*.

O

OPENING HOURS

Banks generally open Mon–Fri 8.30am–1.30pm and 2.45–4pm. Some branches may also be opened on Saturday mornings.

In general, shops open Mon–Sat 9am–1pm and 4–7pm or 8pm, although the big ones now stay open even on Sundays. In resorts, hours will be stretched to fit high season demand. In winter, many shops, even in Naples, simply close for the whole season.

Churches close for most of the afternoon, reopening around 5pm, but the biggest churches may remain open all day. Museum hours vary enormously (consult websites or check with the tourist information offices); most are closed on Mondays or Tuesdays. Ticket offices close one hour before the official closing time. Archaeological sites close one hour before sunset; two hours in the case of Pompeii and Herculaneum.

P

POLICE

In town, the *vigili urbani*, in blue or summer white uniforms with white hats, handle traffic and routine tasks. The *carabinieri*, dressed in brown or black uniforms, maintain law and order. Their headquarters, the Questura, deals with visas and other complaints, and is a good point of reference if you need help. The motorways are patrolled by the *polizia stradale*. Another corps of national police and customs guards are on duty at frontier

Where's the nearest police station? **Dov'è il commissariato di polizia più vicino?**

posts, airports and railway stations. Police HQ, Via Medina 75, Naples; tel: 081-794 1111 (http://questure.poliziadistato.it/Napoli).

In an emergency, dial 112 or 113 for police assistance.

POST OFFICES

Look for the yellow sign with PT in blue. Normal post office hours are 8.30am–5pm Mon–Fri, and 8.30am–noon on Sat. The Naples main post office on Piazza Matteotti is open 8am–6.30pm Mon–Fri, 8am–12.30pm Mon–Sat. Post boxes on the streets are painted red; the slot marked *'Per la Città'* is for local mail, while the other labelled *'Altre Destinazioni'* is for all other destinations. Stamps *(francobolli)* can also be bought at tobacconists and at some hotels. Ask for *Posta Prioritaria* if you want an express service.

> Where's the nearest post office? **Dov'è l' ufficio postale più vicino?**
> A stamp for this letter/postcard, please. **Un francobollo per questa lettera/cartolina, per favore.**
> airmail **via aerea**

R

RELIGION

There is no shortage of daily Roman Catholic services in Naples and the resort communities. In Naples, the Anglican Church at Via San Pasquale 18 in Chiaia (www.christchurchnaples.org) has Sunday services at 10.30am; tel: 081-411842. The Synagogue in Vico Santa Maria a Cappella Vecchia, off Piazza dei Martiri, holds services on Fridays at sunset and at 8.30am on Saturdays; tel: 081-764 3480. For Protestant services in Italian, see the monthly *Qui Napoli* bulletin, available to download from www.inaples.it.

T

TELEPHONE

Most Italians have mobile phones (European standard GSM, so Americans will need a tri- or quad-band phone) so public telephones (*cabina telefonica*) are fairly scarce. It is possibly worth buying a universal SIM card (www.globalsimcard.co.uk) for use while there or a local SIM card from any local telecom shop. However, you can also phone from bars and cafés with an orange telephone sign outside. Overseas calls can be made from any Telecom Italia office called Punto Telecom. In Naples, long-distance calls can be made from the main post office, while on Capri there is a long-distance telephone office (open 8–11.30am and 3–11pm) adjoining the clock tower in the Piazzetta.

Most public telephones only accept phonecards (*scheda telefonica*), available in different denominations from tobacconists and Telecom Italia offices. There are also pre-paid international phone cards, with toll-free numbers for different countries. To make an international call, dial 00, followed by the country code. To phone Italy, the country code is +39.

If you want to make a reverse-charge (collect) call, you must often insert a coin or a card to access a line (even for toll-free calls). Hotels often charge exorbitantly and add service charges' for toll-free calls.

These English-speaking services operate 24 hours a day:

International operator: **170**

International directory enquiries: **176**

TICKETS

Advance tickets for performances and events can often be arranged through hotel concierges or bought at the following agencies:

Box Office: Via San Carlo, 98/F, tel: 081-797 2111; www.teatrosancarlo.it. Tickets for the opera at Teatro San Carlo.

Concerteria: Via M. Schipa 23, Naples; tel: 081-761 1221; www.concerteria.it.

TIME ZONE

Italy follows Central European Time (GMT+1) and from late March to the last weekend in October, clocks are put forward one hour.

> What time is it? **Che ora è?**

TIPPING

A service charge of approximately 15 percent is added to restaurant bills. If prices are quoted as all-inclusive (*tutto compreso* or *servizio incluso*), the service charge is included. In addition to a restaurant's service charge, it is customary to give the waiter something extra, preferably in cash. Porters, doormen, bartenders and service-station attendants all expect a tip. Rounding up your taxi fare to the next euro will satisfy your driver.

> Thank you, this is for you. **Grazie, questo è per Lei.**
> Keep the change. **Tenga il resto.**

TOILETS

Toilets may be labelled with a symbol of a man or a woman or the initials WC. Sometimes the wording will be in Italian: *Uomini* (or *Signori*) is for men, *Donne* (or *Signore*) is for women. Head for the lobby of a large hotel for the cleanest facilities. Always carry a packet of tissues, just in case the toilet is not properly stocked.

> Where are the toilets, please? **Dove sono i gabinetti, per favore?**

TOURIST INFORMATION

The standard symbol for information offices is an '*i*.' All resort towns have one in a central location –just ask for the Ufficio di Turismo. In **Naples**, the main tourist office is in Piazza del Gesù (tel: 081-551 2701). In the Capodichino Airport arrival hall an information desk provides brochures and maps of the city and region. In **Capri** the tiny tourist office is in the belltower at the corner of the town square (tel: 081-837 0686, www.capritourism.com). On **Ischia** it is to the right of the dock at 72 Via Antonio Sogliuzzo (tel: 081-507 4211). In **Positano** it is behind the beachfront cafés at Via del Saracino 4 (tel: 089-875 067). In **Sorrento**, it is near Piazza Tasso at 35 Via L. De Maio (tel: 081-807 4033). **Ravello**'s tourist office is near the main piazza at 18bis Via Roma (tel: 089-857 096).

The Italian State Tourist Offices (ENIT; www.enit.it) are found in Italy and abroad.

Australia and New Zealand: Level 2, 140 William Street, East Sydney, Sydney, NSW 2011; tel: 02 9357 2561; http://sydney.enit.it.

Canada: 69 Yonge St, Suite 1404, Toronto, Ontario M5E 1K3, tel: (416) 925 4882; http://toronto.enit.it.

UK: 1 Princes Street, London W1B 2AY, tel: (020) 7408 1254: http://london.enit.it.

US: 686 Park Ave, New York 10065; tel: 212-245 5618; http://new york.enit.it.

TRANSPORT

Naples and the surrounding bay have an excellent integrated transport network of metros (subways/undergrounds), bus lines, trams, funiculars and suburban railways, as well as ferries and taxis. For information, tel: 800-639525; www.anm.it. Get the integrated transport map and bus timetables from a local tourist information office. Always remember to buy tickets before getting onto buses (from newsagents and tobacconists) and punch the time on all tickets, otherwise you risk a stiff fine.

Bus. 90-minute or all-day tickets valid for unlimited bus, metro and funicular travel are available in Naples (see page 115 for costs). Capri's bus terminal for Anacapri and the two harbours is on Via Roma, just beyond the main square. In Ischia town the round-the-island buses leave from a parking area to the right of the harbour. Tickets may be purchased from ticket offices in the terminals.

Metro and suburban trains. Naples has a rapidly growing metro system, as well as trams, buses and four funiculars that connect the clifftop district of Vomero to the city centre. Stretching out to the north from the Montesanto Station are the Circumflegrea and Cumana lines (www.eavsrl.it) for Pozzuoli and the Phlegrean Fields sites. To the south, the Circumvesuviana line (www.sitabus.it/circumvesuviana-orari-e-tariffe) takes you to Ercolano (Herculaneum), Pompeii and Sorrento from Piazza Garibaldi's Central Station or the dedicated station nearby. You can use metro tickets on the Circumflegrea, but you need a separate ticket for the Circumvesuviana unless you have an inclusive Campania Artecard.

Taxis (*tassi* or taxi). In Naples taxis can be found at a taxi rank, hailed or ordered by telephone. The numbers for all the Naples ranks are in the *Qui Napoli* bulletin and can be called by your hotel or from a restaurant. A flag marked *libero* and a roof light at night indicate free taxis. For long trips out of town, taxis are entitled to charge a double fare for returning empty. Negotiate and confirm before undertaking such a trip, or have your hotel concierge do so. It is normal practice to round up the fare.

Ferries (*traghetti*). Ferries and hydrofoils (*aliscafi*) to the islands, and to Sorrento, the Amalfi coastal towns and Salerno, leave frequently from the Molo Beverello pier at the foot of Piazza Municipio, starting at around 6am until around 9pm. *Il Mattino* publishes a complete timetable daily.

V

VISAS

For a stay of up to three months, a valid passport is sufficient for citizens of Australia, Canada, New Zealand and the US. Visitors from EU countries need only an identity card to enter Italy. Tourists from South Africa must have a visa. Free exchange of non-duty-free goods for personal use is allowed between EU countries.

W

WEBSITES AND INTERNET ACCESS

Naples: Life, Death & Miracles www.naplesldm.com – a true labour of love by an erudite local academic, with masses of historical info and links.

Napoli Unplugged www.napoliunplugged.com – by a knowledgeable local resident.

Naples Tourism www.inaples.it – city's tourism website, with downloadable *Qui Napoli* tourist guide.

Campania Tourism www.regione.campania.it – region's website.

Campania Arte Card www.campaniaartecard.it – the single most useful card for tourists, it is a combination entry ticket, discount card and transport ticket rolled into one.

All hotels offer internet access these days, although most charge for it, but you will find plenty of internet cafés and free Wi-Fi spots in tourist areas (check wifisharing.co/italy/free-wifi-naples).

Y

YOUTH HOSTELS

Naples' one official youth hostel (Ostello Mergellina Napoli, Salita della Grotta 23; tel: 081-7612346) is available for members of the International Youth Hostels Federation. There are also a number of private hostels, best of which is the friendly Hostel of the Sun near the port (Via G. Melisurgo 15; tel: 081-420 6393, www.hostelnapoli.com). You can also find a list of private hostels in and around Naples at www.hostel mancininaples.com.

RECOMMENDED HOTELS

Italian hotels are classified by the government from five stars down to one star according to the facilities they offer, though the star rating does not give a guide to the character or location of the hotel. Prices nearly always include breakfast, but check when you book. As a basic guide we have used the symbols below to indicate prices per night for a double room with bath or shower, including service charge and taxes, during the high season. Prices may be considerably lower in the off-season (generally November to mid-March), although most resort hotels close then. Bear in mind that rooms with sea views generally cost more. In the coastal resorts, it is not unusual to find that half-board is compulsory in high season. All of the hotels listed accept major credit cards except where noted.

€€€€	300 euros and above
€€€	200–300 euros
€€	140–200 euros
€	below 140 euros

NAPLES

Eurostars Excelsior €€€ *Via Partenope 48, tel: +34-902 93 24 24*, www. eurostarsexcelsior.com. This elegant old-timer enjoys a perfect position overlooking the Castel dell'Ovo. The rooms have luxurious linens, sweeping drapes and marble bathrooms, with beautiful views across the bay. There's a fantastic rooftop gourmet restaurant too. 122 rooms and suites.

Exe Majestic €€ *Largo Vasto a Chiaia 68, 80121, tel: 081-416500*, www. exemajestic.com. Set between the Centro Storico and Piazza Plebiscito, this is a very practical place to stay, offering comfort and convenience at a reasonable price but without much romance. It has a good restaurant plus a fitness centre. 112 rooms.

Albergo Palazzo Decumani €€ *Via del Grande Archivio 8, tel: 081-420 1379*, www.palazzodecumani.com. A chic boutique townhouse right in the heart of the Centro Storico, near the Duomo. It offers a plentiful breakfast and has its own bar. No outdoor space, but you are within easy strolling distance of plenty of *caffès*. 28 rooms.

Parker's €€€€ *Corso Vittorio Emanuele 135, 80121, tel: 081-7612474*, www.grandhotelparkers.it. Founded in 1870, this grand hotel is away from the waterfront in fashionable Chiaia. The rooftop George's Restaurant and Bar offers candlelit dining at night, and heart-stopping views of Vesuvius and Capri by day. 82 rooms and suites.

Piazza Bellini €€ *Via S Maria di Costantinopoli 101, 80134, tel: 081-451732*, www.hotelpiazzabellini.com. A small boutique hotel growing up fast, this charming establishment in one of Naples' trendiest piazzas, on the edge of the old city, has spacious, smartly decorated and funky rooms. Staff is delightful and the lovely outdoor lounge area is a plus. 48 rooms.

Santa Lucia €€ *Via Partenope 46, 80121, tel: 081-764 0666*, www.santalucia.it. The picturesque port is the timeless view enjoyed by many of the rooms in one of Naples' loveliest hotels. Directly across from the Castel dell'Ovo. 100 rooms.

Vesuvio €€€€ *Via Partenope 45, 80121, tel: 081-7640044*, www.vesuvio.it. A glorious grande-dame of a hotel with wonderfully spacious rooms, the Vesuvio stares serenely out across Santa Lucia and the bay. The great Neapolitan tenor Caruso was a frequent guest. Sumptuous spa. 181 rooms.

CAPRI

Capri Palace €€€€ *Via Capodimonte 14, Anacapri, tel: 081-978 0111*, www.capripalace.com. Anacapri's seclusion, top-rate beauty and health centre, and a Michelin 2-star restaurant are the magnets at the island's most luxurious hotel. The large pools and lush gardens are highlights; the views, on a clear day, stretch to Mt Vesuvius. 69 rooms. Open year round.

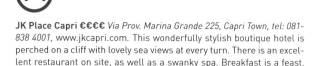

JK Place Capri €€€€ *Via Prov. Marina Grande 225, Capri Town, tel: 081-838 4001*, www.jkcapri.com. This wonderfully stylish boutique hotel is perched on a cliff with lovely sea views at every turn. There is an excellent restaurant on site, as well as a swanky spa. Breakfast is a feast. 22 rooms.

La Minerva €€€ *Via Occhio Marino 8, Capri Town, tel: 081-837 7067*, www.laminervacapri.com. Cascading off the cliff near the Certosa, ten minutes' walk from the centre of Capri Town, this stunning 18-room boutique hotel has a pool, magnificent views, elegant design and good food. A winning combination.

Quisisana €€€€ *Via Camerelle 2, Capri Town, tel: 081-860 0099*, www.quisisana.it. For decades the island's most fabled hotel, this is an oasis in the town centre. Luxurious rooms with sea views, manicured gardens, indoor and outdoor pools, gym, spa and tennis. Outdoor dining. The trendy front-porch bar is perfect for people-watching and a drink. 150 rooms.

Hotel La Tosca € *Via D. Birago 5, Capri Town, tel: 081-837 0989*, www.latoscahotel.com. Hugely popular small hotel in central Capri, with an attentive and knowledgeable host, simple but attractive rooms and wonderful terrace views. 11 rooms.

Villa Sarah €€ *Via Tiberio 3/a, Capri Town, tel: 081-837 7817*, www.villasarahcapri.com. Centrally located yet removed from the hubbub, this is a quiet, clean family-run hotel with contemporary rooms and a beautiful shady garden surrounded by olive and lemon groves. A few rooms on upper floors face the sea. Open from Easter to September. 20 rooms.

ISCHIA

Il Monastero € *Castello Aragonese, Ischia Ponte, tel: 081-992435*, www.albergoilmonastero.it. Old monastery within the Castello Aragonese converted into a good-value *pensione*. Rooms are simple but attractive, some of them opening on to the terrace, with stunning sea views. Good restaurant. Open April to October. 22 rooms.

Hotel Terme Aragona Palace €€€€ *Via Porto 12, Ischia Porto, tel: 081-333 1229*, www.hotelaragona.it. Right on the harbourfront in Ischia Porto, this modern hotel, decked out in cool island blue and white, has friendly staff, spacious rooms, a pool, restaurant and, inevitably on Ischia, a spa. 40 rooms.

Terme Manzi Hotel and Spa €€€ *Piazza Bagni 4, Casamicciola Terme, tel: 081-994 722*, www.termemanzihotel.com. Luxurious purpose-built hotel and cutting-edge spa at the foot of Mt Epomeo. It is set in lovely gardens, with fabulous sea views and a private beach, a few minutes' walk from the village of Casamicciola Bassa. Home to the two Michelin star Il Mosaico restaurant. 61 rooms.

Hotel Terme San Michele €€€ *Via Sant'Angelo 60, Sant'Angelo, tel: 081-999276*, www.hoteltermesanmichele.it. A shady oasis surrounds this modern waterside hotel with a large pool, pretty gardens, shady terraces, and a full-scale beauty centre for thermal water and mud treatments. Tasteful guest rooms, many with balconies and sea views. Half board in the busy restaurant is compulsory. Open April to October. 42 rooms.

SORRENTO

La Badia € *Via Nastro Verde 8, Sorrento, tel: 081-878 1154*, www.hotellabadia.it. A delightful little restored abbey surrounded by citrus groves, on the clifftops above Sorrento town. Pool, restaurant and fabulous views. It is a steep walk but there are regular buses. 41 rooms.

Grand Hotel Excelsior Vittoria €€€€ *Piazza Tasso 34, tel: 081-877 7111*, www.exvitt.it. An elegant cliff-top Belle Epoque dream, awash with *trompe l'oeil*, potted plants, and gorgeous views over Vesuvius and the bay. This lovely small hotel was once home to the great Caruso (with his suite available for special bookings). Secluded but in the very heart of town, with a semi-tropical garden, large swimming pool, and a lift to take bathers down to the sea. Formal indoor and terraced alfresco restaurant with views, coupled with a holistic spa. 84 rooms.

Imperial Tramontano €€€ *Via Vittorio Veneto 1, tel: 081-878 2588,* www.hoteltramontano.it. Parts of this villa-like hotel date from the 15th century. Perched on a cliff and surrounded by subtropical gardens, it has a freshwater swimming pool, and spacious ceramic-tiled rooms, some with superb views of the Bay of Naples. Private beach and a restaurant run by master-chef, Alfonso Iaccarino. Open March to December. 113 rooms.

La Tonnarella €€ *Via del Capo 31, tel: 081-878 1153,* www.latonnarella.com. This clifftop villa is good value, and one of only a few on the coast open all year. A quiet hideaway, yet only a 10-minute walk into town. A few rooms have pine-shaded terracotta balconies and panoramic bay views. Small private pebble beach (with bar) is reached by a lift. Excellent restaurant. 24 rooms.

POSITANO

Casa Albertina €€€ *Via della Tavolozza 3, tel: 089-875143,* www.casalbertina.it. This pretty family-owned guesthouse is not for the weak of knee: there are 300 steps down to the beach, but it has exceptional views. Some rooms with balconies and Jacuzzis. Compulsory half-board in high season. 20 rooms.

Covo dei Saraceni €€€€ *Via Regina Giovanna 5, tel: 089-875400,* www.covodeisaraceni.it. If you were any closer to the sea you would be in it. Rather luxe, this long-time favourite has cool, stylish rooms with seaview balconies, many with Jacuzzis. A delightful rooftop pool and bar and a fine terrace restaurant. 66 rooms.

Palazzo Murat €€€€ *Via dei Mulini 23, tel: 089-875177,* www.palazzomurat.it. Elegant and romantic town-centre hotel in a 19th-century palazzo furnished with antiques. A quiet subtropical courtyard surrounds the slightly cheaper Mediterranean-style wing. Good restaurant (dinner only). Open mid-March to early January. 32 rooms.

Hotel Pasitea €€€ *Viale Pasitea 207, tel: 089-875 500,* www.hotelpasitea.it. A cool and comfortable hotel halfway up the cliff with wonderful views, friendly staff, comfortable if relatively simple rooms, its own art gallery and wine bar. B&B and snacks only, but the staff is happy to recommend some excellent local restaurants. One of very few hotels in town to stay open all year. 61 rooms. Open mid-March to early January.

Poseidon €€€€ *Via Pasitea 148, tel: 089-811111,* www.hotelposeidon positano.it. The Aonzo family proudly runs this hillside hotel, one of Positano's most pleasant and popular. Removed from the day-tripping buzz yet accessible to everything, it has a pool, beauty centre, gym and good restaurant. All rooms have terraces and lovely views. 48 rooms. Open early April to 6 January.

San Pietro €€€€ *Via Laurito 2, tel: 089 812 080,* www.ilsanpietro.it. An A-listers' hideaway with a dozen levels of vine-covered balconies chiselled into the cliff above a private helipad, this stunning, secluded family-owned hotel offers a mix of refined elegance and airy, contemporary decor. Stylish restaurant, spa, small and rocky private beach. Open April to October. 62 rooms.

Le Sirenuse €€€€ *Via C. Colombo 30, tel: 089-875066,* www.sirenuse.it. In an aristocratic 18th-century building in town above the beach, this is one of the country's most special hotels. Museum-quality family heirlooms throughout, wonderful open views of the sea and town, stylish health centre, outdoor pool and refined restaurant. 58 rooms.

AMALFI

Marina Riviera €€€€ *Via P. Comite 19, tel: 089-871 104,* www.marina riviera.it. An impeccably run 4-star hotel set on a cliff overlooking the sea. Some of the rooms have been given a glamorous makeover, while others have a breezy, seaside feel. The beach is a short stroll away, and there is a pool on the roof. A gourmet restaurant, Eolo, completes the picture. Open end March to early November.

Santa Caterina €€€€ *Strada Amalfitana 9, tel: 089-871012,* www.hotel santacaterina.it. Owned by the same family for generations, this is another of the coast's venerable hotels, carved into multiple levels of a cliff. Old-world and comfortably elegant, the hotel has a saltwater pool, lush terraced gardens, glorious views, a small private beach and respected restaurant – all further enhanced by warm, helpful staff. An easy walk from town, or there is a convenient shuttle service. 66 rooms and suites.

Villa Lara Hotel €€ *Via delle Cartiere 1, tel: 089-873 6358*, www.villalara. it. A converted 19th-century villa on the cliff above the town, with a private lift from the centre, this charming little hotel is surrounded by lemon groves and offers breathtaking sea views and good value.

RAVELLO

Belmond Caruso €€€€ *Via San Giovanni del Toro 2, tel: 089-858 801*, www. belmond.com/hotel-caruso-amalfi-coast. This 11th-century aristocratic home is now a super-luxe hotel in a gorgeous cliff-top setting. One of the most elegant hotels around. Rooms are expensive, but they have breathtaking sea views and are worth the premium. The food at the Belvedere restaurant is magnificent. 50 rooms. Open Easter to early November.

Villa Cimbrone €€€€ *Via Santa Chiara 26, tel: 089-857459*, www.villa cimbrone.com. The suite Greta Garbo stayed in is part of this magical old palazzo. Vaulted, frescoed rooms filled with an eclectic mix of antiques belonging to the former British owner's family. The enchanting gardens suspended above the sea are for hotel guests alone once the grounds close at dusk. Located at the end of a 15-minute trek along a charming footpath; porters will help guests with luggage. There is a Michelin-star restaurant too. Open April to October. 19 rooms.

INDEX

Berlitz pocket guide

NAPLES, CAPRI
& THE AMALFI COAST

Thirteenth Edition 2017

Editor: Carine Tracanelli
Author: Natasha Foges
Updater: Maciej Zglinicki
Head of Production: Rebeka Davies
Picture Editor: Tom Smyth
Cartography Update: Carte
Update Production: Apa Digital
Photography Credits: Chris Coe/Apa
Publications 15; 45, 92; Dreamstime 71, 86;
Getty Images 4TL, 7, 11; Greg Gladman/Apa
Publications 4TC, 4MC, 5T, 5M, 6L, 6R, 7R,
17, 22, 25, 26, 28, 31, 33, 34, 36, 39, 41, 43, 47,
48, 51, 55, 57, 58, 61, 63, 65, 67, 68, 73, 74, 77,
79, 80, 84, 94, 99, 100, 102, 104; iStock 1, 5TC,
5MC, 13, 19, 20, 53, 83, 90; Phil Wood/Apa
Publications 88; Shutterstock 4ML, 5M, 5MC
Cover Picture: Shutterstock

Distribution

UK, Ireland and Europe: Apa Publications
(UK) Ltd; sales@insightguides.com
United States and Canada: Ingram
Publisher Services; ips@ingramcontent.com
Australia and New Zealand: Woodslane;
info@woodslane.com.au
Southeast Asia: Apa Publications (SN) Pte;
singaporeoffice@insightguides.com
Hong Kong, Taiwan and China:
Apa Publications (HK) Ltd;
hongkongoffice@insightguides.com
Worldwide: Apa Publications (UK) Ltd;
sales@insightguides.com

**Special Sales, Content Licensing
and CoPublishing**
Insight Guides can be purchased in bulk
quantities at discounted prices. We can
create special editions, personalised jackets
and corporate imprints tailored to your
needs. sales@insightguides.com;
www.insightguides.biz

Contact us
Every effort has been made to provide
accurate information in this publication,
but changes are inevitable. The publisher
cannot be responsible for any resulting loss,
inconvenience or injury. We would appreciate
it if readers would call our attention to any
errors or outdated information. We also
welcome your suggestions; please contact
us at: berlitz@apaguide.co.uk
www.insightguides.com/berlitz

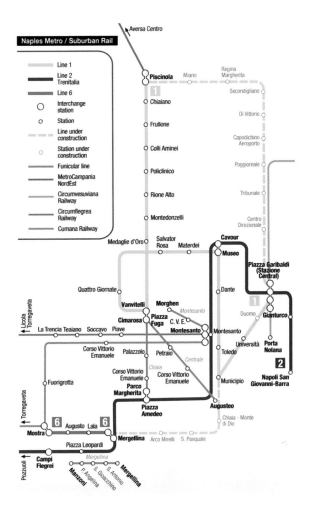

Berlitz®

speaking your language

phrase book & dictionary
phrase book & CD

Available in: Arabic, Brazilian Portuguese*, Burmese*, Cantonese Chinese, Croatian, Czech*, Danish*, Dutch, English, Filipino, Finnish*, French, German, Greek, Hebrew*, Hindi*, Hungarian*, Indonesian, Italian, Japanese, Korean, Latin American Spanish, Malay, Mandarin Chinese, Mexican Spanish, Norwegian, Polish, Portuguese, Romanian*, Russian, Spanish, Swedish, Thai, Turkish, Vietnamese
*Book only